Eliza B. Burnz

Liberal Hymn Book

a collection of liberal songs adapted to popular tunes - for use in liberal

leagues and other meetings, and in liberal homes

Eliza B. Burnz

Liberal Hymn Book
*a collection of liberal songs adapted to popular tunes - for use in liberal leagues and
other meetings, and in liberal homes*

ISBN/EAN: 9783337265823

Printed in Europe, USA, Canada, Australia, Japan

Cover: Foto ©Thomas Meinert / pixelio.de

More available books at **www.hansebooks.com**

THE

LIBERAL HYMN BOOK.

A COLLECTION OF

LIBERAL SONGS

ADAPTED TO POPULAR TUNES.

FOR USE IN LIBERAL LEAGUES AND OTHER
MEETINGS, AND IN LIBERAL HOMES.

Edited by
ELIZA BOARDMAN BURNZ.

The one, sole, sacred thing beneath the cope of heven is MAN.
WHITTIER.

*Let me make the ballads of a people and I care not who
makes the laws.*—ANDREW FLETCHER, 1667.

NEW YORK:
BURNZ & CO., PUBLISHERS,
24 CLINTON PLACE,
1880.

To the

SPIRIT OF FREE INQUIRY,

which seeks, earnestly yet reverently, for knowledge on all subjects pertaining to human Existence, Welfare and Progres, this book of Liberal Songs is trustfully dedicated.

PREFACE.

This collection of Liberal Songs is offered to the frends of free thought in the belief that such a book is needed and that it wil\ be acceptable.

At the present day Music constitutes no inconsiderable portion of the entertainment usually provided for social and religious meetings, and there is no reason why Liberals should not strengthen and encourage themselves and their brethren by the sweet voice of song, while they at the same time attract others to their communion. To omit to sing liberal songs, is to neglect a very effective means for extending the domain of free thought.

Altho' the songs in this book ar of very varied character, it has been the aim of the compiler to introduce no song objectionable in either spirit or words to that broad and generous Liberalism which regards the beliefs of the past as steps by which humanity has ascended; and which, consequently, tho' open to criticism from our present standpoint, ar unfit subjects for sneers and vituperation.

Every verse of the "Songs of Standard Poets" is given without alteration, as it appears in the authorized editions of the works of each poet. Many of the "Songs to Popular Tunes," and some of those which follow, ar materially modified; some in sentiment, some in measure, some in length. The author's name is appended wherever known, and if the verses ar considerably changed the word " adapted " is added. Many excellent poems ar omitted because they cannot be sung to any wel-known tune. In the first half of the book a suitable tune is suggested for each song. In the latter half, when the meter is given without a tune, the musical leader of the occasion can select some tune named in connection with previous songs which hav the same mesure.

It is fitting that a book publisht especially for the frends of Progres, should be printed in simplified spelling. Persons who hav expanding minds, which forbid their clinging too closely to old forms of any kind, wil surely look with tolerance, if not with decided favor upon the few reformed spellings here introduced, altho' they do change, unavoidably, the familiar appearance of some words. The alterations ar made by the omission of a few useles letters, and ar in accordance

with the five rules of the American Spelling Reform Association slightly modified.

1. Omit *a* from the digraf *ea* when pronounst as *e*-short, as in hed, helth, etc.

2, Omit silent *e* after a short vowel, as in hav, giv, activ, etc., except words ending in *ce*.

3. Write *f* for *ph* in such words as alfabet, fantom, etc.

4. When a word ends with a double letter, after the regular short sounds of *a*, *e*, *i*, *o*, *u*, omit the last, as in shal, clif, eg, etc.

5, Change *ed* final to *t* when it has the sound of *t*, as in lasht, imprest, etc., except after *ce*,

The observance of these five rules does
not make our orthography fonetic, nor
wil the new spellings of derived words be
found in all cases consistant; it is simply
desired, by means of these few simplified
spellings, to call public attention to the
fact that a revision of our "monstrous
orthography" is in progres, and also to
accustom readers of these songs to some
of those fonetic spellings which wil un-
doubtedly form part of English orthog-
rafy when it is fully revised.

Criticisms, corrections of errors, the
supplying of omissions, and contributions
of other suitable hymns which can be
added to a second edition, wil be accep-
ted with plesure.

Eliza B. Burnz.

24 Clinton Place N. Y.

CONTENTS.

LIBERAL SONGS

ADAPTED TO POPULAR TUNES.

Songs by Standard Poets,

—o—

1.   THE OLD AND NEW.

L. M. *Tune—Old Hundred.*

O, sometimes gleams upon our sight,
Through present wrong, the eternal right!
And step by step since time began,
We see the stedy gain of man.

Whate'er of good the past has had,
Remains to make our own time glad;
Our common daily life divine,
And every land a Palestine.

Through the harsh noises of the day
A low sweet prelude finds its way;
Through clouds of dout and creeds of fear
A light is breaking, calm and clear.

Henceforth my heart shal sigh no more
For olden time and holier shore;
God's* love and blesing, then and there,
Ar now and here and everywhere.

Whittier.

---

* NOTE.—The word " God " designates any man's

2.   ALL MEN AR EQUAL.

C. M. *Tune—Warwick.*

All men ar equal in their birth,
　Heirs of the earth and skies,
All men ar equal when that earth
　Fades from their dying eyes.

All wait alike on him, whose power
　Upholds the life he gave;
The sage within his starry tower,
　The savage in his cave.

'Tis man alone who difference sees,
　And speaks of high and low;
Who worships those and tramples these
　While the same path they go.

Ye great ! renounce your earth-born
　　　pride ;
Ye low ! your shame and fear;
Liv, as ye worship, side by side ;
　Your common claims revere.

Harriet Martineau.

---

highest conception of the Great First Cause—The Power or force that brought himself and the Universe into being. This unknown yet evident and all-prevading Power may be personified, or spoken of and addrest, with as much propriety as Wisdom, Truth, etc., and perhaps no word can be employed that is more significant and appropriate than " God." For " God " means " Good " and Life itself is good. " It is a pleasant thing to behold the Sun." *Editor.*

3. O YET WE TRUST.

L. M. *Tune—Rockingham.*

O yet we trust that somehow good
Wil be the final goal of il,
To pangs of nature, sins of wil,
Defects of dout, and taints of blood.

Behold we know not anything;
We can but trust that good shal fall
At last—far off—at last, to all,
And every winter change to spring.

Tennyson.

4. SEED-TIME AND HARVEST.

L. M. *Tune—Hebron.*

As o'er his furrowed fields, which lie
Beneath a coldly-dropping sky,
Yet chil with winter's melted snow;
The husbandman goes forth to sow.

Thus, Freedom, on the bitter blast,
The ventures of thy seed we cast,
And trust to warmer sun and rain,
To swel the germs and fil the grain.

Who calls thy glorious service hard?
Who deems it not its own reward?
Who, for its trials, counts it les,
A cause of praise and thankfulnes?

It may not be our lot to wield
The sickle in the ripened field;
Nor ours to hear, on summer eves,
The reaper's song among the sheaves;

Yet, where our duty's task is wrought,
In unison with all great thought,
The near and future blend in one,
And whatsoe'er is willed, is done.

Whittier.

5.   WHOM TO HONOR.

8, 7. *Tune--Sicilian Hymn.*

Honor him whose hands ar sowing
　　Seed for harvest in their time—
Reverence those whose thoughts ar
　　　　growing
　　Up to ultimates sublime.

All the progres of the ages
　　May be traced back to their hands—
All th' illuminated pages
　　Of the books, into their plans.

Lo, the humble flower that's lying
　　In your pathway, may contain
Some elixir, which the dying
　　Generation sought in vain.

In the stone that waits the turning
　　Of some curious hand from sight,
Fiery atoms may be burning,
　　That would fil the world with light.

Let us then, in reverence bowing,
　　Honor most of all mankind,
Such as keep their great thoughts plow-
　　　ing,
Deepest in the field of mind.

　　　　　　　　　　　　　　　Alice Carey.

6,　　　　THE BUILDERS.

　　　7s. *Tune—Pleyel's Hymn.*

All ar architects of fate
　　Working in these walls of Time;
Some with massive deeds and great,
　　Some with ornaments of rhyme.

Nothing useles is or low,
　　Each thing in its place is best;
And what seems but idle show
　　Strengthens and supports the rest.

For the structure that we raise,
　　Time is with materials filled;
Our to-days and yesterdays
　　Ar the blocks with which we build.

Build to-day then strong and sure,
　　With a firm and ample base;
And ascending and secure
　　Shal to-morrow find its place.

　　　　　　　　　　　　　　　Longfellow.

7.   FRENDS OF FREEDOM.

P. M. *Tune—Bruce's Address.*

Frends of freedom! ye who stand,
With no wepon in your hand,
Save a purpose stern and grand,
    All men to set free:
Welcome! Freedom stands in need
Of true men in thought and deed—
Men who hav this only creed,
    That they wil not flee.

Though we ar but two or three,
Sure of triumf we should be;
We our promist land shal see,
    Though the way seems long;
Every fearles word we speak
Makes sin's stronghold bend and creak—
Tyranny is always weak,
    Truth is always strong.

All the hero-spirits vast,
Who hav sanctified the past,
Bearing witnes to the last,
    Fight upon our part;
We can never be forlorn;
He who in a manger born,
Bore the priest's and Levite's scorn,
    Givs us hope and heart.

                    James Russell Lowell.

8. THE LADDER OF LIFE.

L. M. *Tune—Duke Street.*

SAINT AUGUSTINE, wel hast thou said,
  That of our vices we can frame
A ladder, if we wil but tred.
  Beneath our feet each deed of shame.

All common things, each day's events
  That with the hour begin and end,
Our plesures and our discontents,
  Ar rounds by which we may ascend.

We hav not wings, we cannot soar,
  But we hav feet to scale and climb
By slow degrees, by more and more,
  The cloudy summits of our time.

The hights by great men reacht and
      kept,
  Were not attained by sudden flight,
But they, while their companions slept,
  Were toiling upward in the night.

Standing on what too long we bore
  With shoulders bent and down cast eyes,
We may discern—unseen before,
  A path to higher destinies.

Longfellow.

9,   BENEVOLENCE.

C. M. *Tune—Heber.*

Blest is the man whose generous heart
    Feels all another's pain;
To whom the supplicating eye
    Is never raised in vain.

Whose brest expands with generous
      warmth,
    A brother's woes to feel,
And bleeds in pity o'er the wound
    He wants the power to heal.

He spreds his kind, supporting arms
    To every child of grief;
His secret bounty largely flows,
    And brings unaskt relief.

To gentle offices of love
    His feet ar never slow;
He views, through mercy's melting eye,
    A brother in a foe.
                Mrs. Barbauld.

10.   STAND FIRMLY.

8, 7. *Tune—Autumn.*

There ar moments when life's shadows
    Fall all darkly on the soul,
Hiding stars of hope behind them
    In a black impervious scroll;

When we walk with trembling footsteps,
  Scarcely knowing how or where
The dim paths we tred ar leading,
  In our midnight of despair!

Stand we firm, in that dred moment,
  Stand we firm, nor shrink away;
Looking boldly through the darknes,
  Wait the coming of the day;
Gathering strength while we ar waiting
  For the conflict yet to come;
Fear not, fail not, light wil lead us
  Yet in safety to our home.

Firmly stand—though sirens lure us,
  Firmly stand—though falsehood rail,
Holding justice, truth and mercy,
  Die we may—but cannot fail;
Fail!—it is the word of cowards,
  Fail!—the language of the slave;
Firmly stand til duty beckons;
  Onward then, e'en to the grave.

Frances D. Gage.

11. THE FAITH OF LOVE.

L. M. *Tune—Federal Street.*

What is it, that the crowd requite
  Thy love with hate, thy truth with lies?
And, but to faith and not to sight,
  The walls of Freedom's temple rise.

Yet do thy work; it shal sucseed
   In thine or in another's day;
And if denied the victor's meed,   ·
   Thou shalt not lack the toiler's pay.

Faith shares the future's promise; Love's
   Self-offering is a triumf won;
And each good thought or action moves
   The dark world nearer to the Sun.

Then faint not, falter not, nor plead
   Thy weaknes; truth itself is strong;
The lions's strength, the eagle's speed,
   Ar not alone vouchsaft to wrong.

Whittier.

---

12.   THE UNITY OF LOVE.

C. M. *Tune—Ortonville.*

O Love! O Life! Our faith and sight
   Thy presence maketh one,
As thro' transfigured clouds of white,
   We trace the noon-day sun.

We faintly hear, we dimly see;
   In differing frase we pray;
But, dim or clear, we own in thee,
   The Light, the Truth, the Way!

To do thy wil is more than praise,
   As words ar les than deeds;

And simple trust can find thy ways,
    We mis with chart of creeds.

Alone, O Love ineffable!
    Thy saving name is given;
To turn aside from thee is hel,
    To walk with thee is heven.

Whittier.

---

13.   SUNSHINE.

C. M. *Tune—Swanwick.*

I love the sunshine ev'rywhere—
    In wood, and field, and glen;
I love it in the busy haunts
    Of town-imprisoned men.

I love it when it streameth in
    The humble cottage door,
And casts the checkered casement shade
    Upon the red brick floor.

I love it where the children lie
    Deep in the clov'ry grass,
To watch among the twining roots
    The gold-green beetle pass.

Oh yes! I love the sunshine bright!
    Like kindnes or like mirth
Upon a human countenance,
    Is sunshine on the earth.

Upon the earth—upon the sea—
   And through the crystal air—
On piled up clouds, the gracious sun
   Is glorious ev'rywhere.   *Mary Howitt.*

---

14.   PEACE OF MIND.

Tune—Bonnie Doon.

My mind to me a kingdom is;
   Such perfect joy therein I find,
As far exceeds all earthly blis,
   That God or nature hath assigned.
‖: Tho' much I want that most would hav,
Yet stil my mind forbids to crave. :‖

Content I liv, this is my stay;
   I seek no more than may suffice;
I pres to bear no haughty sway;
   Look, what I lack my mind supplies.
‖: Lo! thus I triumf like a king,
Content with what my mind doth bring. :‖

I laugh not at another's loss,
   I grudge not at another's gain;
No worldly wave my mind can toss;
   I brook that is another's bane.
‖: I fear no foe, nor fawn no frend;
I loathe not life, nor dred my end. :‖

My welth is helth and perfect ease;
   My conscience clear, my chief defence;
I never seek by bribes to please,
   Nor by desert to giv offence.
‖: Thus do I liv, thus wil I die;
Would all did so as wel as I! :‖
        Henry Wotton.

15. A HAPPY LIFE.

Tune—Duane Street.

How happy is he born and taught,
That serveth not another's wil;
Whose armor is his honest thought,
And simple truth his utmost skil;
Whose passions not his masters ar;
Whose soul is stil prepared for deth;
Untied unto the world by care
Of public fame, or private breth.

Who hath his life from rumors freed;
Whose conscience is his strong retreat;
Whose state can neither flatterers feed,
Nor ruin, make oppressors great.
This man is freed from servil bands
Of hope to rise or tear to fall;
Lord of himself, though not of lands,
And having nothing, yet hath all.

Henry Wotton.

---

16. PSALM OF LIFE.

8, 7. *Tune—Autumn.*

Tel me not in mournful numbers
Life is but an empty dream!
For the soul is ded that slumbers,
And things ar not what they seem.

Life is real! Life is earnest!
And the grave is not its goal;
Dust thou art, to dust returnest,
Was not spoken of the soul.

Not enjoyment, and not sorrow,
　Is our destined end and way;
But to act, that each to-morrow
　Find us further than to-day.

Let us then be up and doing,
　With a heart for any fate;
Stil achieving, stil pursuing,
　Learn to Labor and to wait.
Longfellow.

17.　A DAY OF SUNSHINE.

L. M. *Tune—Retreat.*

O gift of God! O perfect day,
Whereon should no man work but play.
Whereon it is enough for me,
Not to be doing but to be!

Through every fiber of my brain,
Through every nerve, thro' every vein,
I feel th' electric thril, the tuch
Of life, that seems almost too much.

I hear the wind among the trees
Playing celestial symfonies;
I see the branches downward bent,
Like keys of some great instrument.

And over me unrolls on high,
The splendid scenery of the sky,
Where, thro' a saffire sea, the sun
Sails like a golden galleon.

O Life and Love, O happy throng
Of thoughts, whose only speech is song!
O heart of man! canst thou not be
Blithe as the air is, and as free?
                          Longfellow.

---

18.   THE LIGHT OF STARS.

C. M.   *Tune—Manoah.*

Within my brest there is no light
   But the cold light of stars;
I giv the first watch of the night
   To the red planet, Mars.

The star of the unconquerd wil,
   He rises in my brest
Serene, and resolute, and stil,
   And calm and self-possest.

O Star of strength! I see thee stand
   And smile upon my pain;
Thou beck'nest with thy mailéd hand,
   And I am strong again.

And thou too whosoe'er thou art,
   That readeth this brief psalm,
As one by one thy hopes depart,
   Be resolute and calm.

O fear not in a world like this,
   And thou shalt know erelong—
Know how sublime a thing it is,
   To suffer and bo strong.
                          Longfellow.

19. MIGHT WITH THE RIGHT.

May ev'ry year but draw more near
    The time when strife shal cease,
When truth and love all hearts shal move
    To liv in joy and peace.
Now sorrow reigns, and earth complains,
For folly stil her cause maintains,
    But the day shal yet appear,
When the might with the right, and the
        truth shal be,
    And come what may to stand in the way,
That day the world shal see.

Though interest pleads that noble deeds,
    The world wil not regard,
To noble minds, when duty binds,
    No sacrifice is hard.
In vain and long, enduring wrong,
The weak may strive against the strong
                But the day. etc.

Let good men ne'er of truth despair,
    Though humble efforts fail;
Oh giv not o'er, until once more
    The righteous cause prevail.
The brave—the true, may seem but few,
But hope has better things in view,
    And the day shal yet appear,
When the might with the right, and the
        truth shal be,
    And come what there may to stand in
        the way,
That day the world shal see.
                                Charles Mackay.

20. THE TRUE FREEMAN.

7s. Tune—Ives.

Men ! Whose boast it is that ye
Come of fathers brave and free,
If there breathe on earth a slave,
Ar ye truly free and brave ?
If ye do not feel the chain,
When it works a brother's pain,
Ar ye not base slaves indeed,—
Slaves unworthy to be freed?

They ar slaves who fear to speak
For the fallen and the weak ;
They ar slaves who wil not choose
Hatred, scoffing, and abuse,
Rather than in silence shrink
From the truth they needs must think;
They ar slaves who dare not be
In the right with two or three.

Lowell.

21. THE BATTLE FIELD.

L. M. Tune—Duke Street.

Ah ! never shal the land forget
How gusht the life-blood of her brave ;
Gusht, warm with hope and valor yet,
Upon the soil they fought to save.

Soon rested those who fought—but thou,
Who minglest in the harder strife
For truths which men receive not now—
Thy warfare only ends with life.

A frendless warfare! lingering long
　　Thro' weary day and weary year;
A wild and many weponed-throng
　　Hang on thy front, and flank, and rear.

Yet nerve thy spirit to the proof,
　　And blench not at thy chosen lot!
The timid good may stand aloof,
　　The sage may frown—yet faint thou not.

Nor heed the shaft too surely cast,
　　The hissing, stinging bolt of scorn;
For, with thy side shal dwel at last,
　　The victory of endurance born.

Truth crusht to earth shal rise again;
　　Th' eternal years of God ar hers;
But Error, wounded, writhes with pain,
　　And dies among his worshipers.

Bryant.

22.　THE CENTRAL SUN.

C. M. *Tune—Ortonville.*

The douts we vainly seek to solve,
　　The truths we know, ar one;
The known and nameles stars revolve
　　Around the central Sun.

And if we reap as we hav sown,
　　And take the dole we deal,
The law of pain is love alone,
　　The wounding is to heal.

O fearful heart and trubled brain!
  Take hope and strength from this,—
That Nature never hints in vain,
  Nor profesies amis.

Her wild birds sing the same sweet stave,
  Her lights and airs ar given
Alike to play-ground and the grave;
  And over both is heven.

Whittier.

---

23.   IN MEMORIAM.

L. M. *Tune—Federal Street.*

Perplext in faith, but pure in deeds,
  At last he beat his music out.
  There is more faith in honest dout,
Believe me, than in half the creeds.

He fought his douts and gatherd strength,
  He would not make his judgment blind,
  He faced the specters of the mind,
And laid them: thus he came at length

To find a stronger faith his own;
  And Power was with him in the night,
  Which makes the darknes and the light,
And dwels not in the light alone.

Tennyson.

24.   FAR OFF, BUT NIGH.

L. M. *Tune—Hebron.*

Thy voice is on the rolling air;
  I hear thee where the waters run;
  Thou standest in the rising sun,
And in the setting thou art fair.

What art thou then? I cannot gues;
  But tho' I seem in star and flower
  To feel thee some diffusiv power,
I do not therefore love thee les.

My love involvs the love before;
  My love is vaster passion now;
  Tho' mixt with God and Nature thou,
I seem to love thee more and more.

Far off thou art but ever nigh:
  I hav thee stil and I rejoice;
  I prosper, circled by thy voice;
I shal not lose thee though I die.

Tennyson.

25.   LOVE.

L. M.   *Tune—Herald.*

Love is and was my Lord and King,
  And in his presence I attend
  To hear the tidings of my frend,
Which every hour his couriers bring.

Love is and was my King and Lord,
  And will be tho' as yet I keep

Within his court on earth, and sleep
Encompast by his faithful guard.

I hear at times a sentinel,
  Who moves about from place to place,
  And whispers to the world of space,
In the deep night, that all is wel.

                     Tennyson.

---

26. SEARCH THINE OWN HEART.

L. M. *Tune—Retreat.*

He loathed the false, yet lived not true
To half the glorious truths he knew ;
The dout, the discord, and the sin,
He mourned without, he felt within.

Midst yearnings for a higher life,
Without were fears, within was strife ;
And stil his wayward act denied
The perfect good for which he sighed.

Alas !—the blows for error ment,
Too oft on truth itself ar spent,
As through the false and vile and base
Looks out her sad rebuking face.

Search thy own heart. What paineth thee
In others, in thyself may be ;
All dust is frail, all flesh is weak ;
Be thou the true man thou doest seek.

                     Whittier.

27. SLEEP SWEETLY.

L. M. *Tune—Malvern.*

Sleep sweetly, tender heart, in peace;
  Sleep, holy spirit, blessed soul,
While the stars burn, the moons increase,
  And the great ages onward roll.

Sleep til the end, true soul and sweet.
  Nothing comes to thee new or strange.
Sleep, full of rest from hed to feet;
  Lie stil, dry dust, secure of change.

                   Tennyson.

28. ' FREND OF MY SOUL.

L. M. *Tune—Hamburg.*

While day by day our loved ones glide
  In spectral silence, husht and lone,
To the cold shadows which divide
  The living from the dred Unknown;

And only, midst the gloom of deth,
  Its mournful douts and haunting fears,
Two pale, sweet angels, Hope and Faith,
  Smile dimly on us thro' their tears.

'Tis something to a heart like mine
  To think of thee as living yet;
To feel that such a light as thine
  Could not in utter darknes set.

O sweetly here upon thee grew
  The lesson which earth's beauty gave,
Th' ideal of the Pure and True
  In earth and sky and gliding wave.

And it may be that all which lends
  The soul an upward impulse here,
With a diviner beauty blends
  And greets us in a holier sfere.

Whittier.

29. A UNIVERSAL PRAYER.

C. M. *Tune—Devizes.*

Father of all, in every age,
  In every clime adored,
By saint, by savage and by sage,
  Jehovah, Jove, or Lord.

Thou great First Cause, least under-
    stood,
  Who all my sense confined,
To know but this—that thou art good
  And that myself am blind;

Yet gave me, in this dark estate,
  To see the good from il;
And binding nature fast in fate,
  Left free the human wil.

What conscience dictates to be done,
  Or warns me not to do,
This, teach me more than hel to shun,
  That, more than heven pursue.

If I am right, thy strength impart
  Stil in the right to stay;
If I am wrong, O teach my heart
  To find the better way.

To thee, whose temple is all space,
  Whose altar, earth, sea, skies,
One chorus let all beings raise,
  All Nature's incense rise.

Pope.

30.   HOME SWEET HOME.

'Mid plesures and palaces tho' we may
  roam,
Be it ever so humble, there's no place
  like home,
A charm from the sky seems to hallow
  us there.
Which seek through the world is not
  met with elswhere.
      Home, home, sweet, sweet home,
      There's no place like home, there's
        no place like home.

An exile from home, splendor dazzles in
  vain,
Oh, giv me my lowly thatch'd cottage
  again!
The birds singing gaily that came at my
  call;
Giv me peace of mind, that is dearer
  than all.
      Home, home, sweet, sweet home, etc.

J. Howard Payne.

Songs to Popular Tunes.

31. SWEET BY AND BY.

We believe in the dawn of a day,
   When the spirit of man shal be free
From the gloom that hangs over his way,
   From the fear of the dredful "to be."
      CHORUS.
   In the sweet by and by,
      We shal fear not the dredful "to be"
   In the sweet by and by,
      It is coming for you and for me.

We have faith that the angel of love,
   Wil destroy every demon of fear,
And the bright sun of science above,
   Wil dispel every ghost that is near.
      CHORUS.

We hav hope that the love of the truth,
   In humanity's bosom wil glow;
So that men whether old or in youth,
   May speak freely not fearing a blow.
      CHORUS.

We rejoice in the dawn of that day;
   It is coming—we see it afar;
Men ar waking, and soon they wil say,
   Truth alone is our bright guiding star.
      CHORUS.

Eliza B. Burnz.

32.   LIBERTY OR DETH.

Tune—Hold the Fort.
Second four lines same music as the Chorus.

Ring again the war-cry sterling,
  As in days of yore,
When her banner truth unfurling,
  Woke the sea and shore.
Let it wake the slumbering nations,
  With its vital breth,
Til they join the aspiration,
  Liberty or deth.
CHORUS. Cry aloud, and wake the nations.
    Spare not voice or breth;
    Cry aloud for truth and freedom,
    Liberty or deth.

Freedom for the mind and spirit,
  For the thoughtful brain;
Freedom that we may inherit,
  Truths that conquer pain.
Freedom that investigation,
  Deepning with each breth,
Wake the soul's great aspiration,
  Liberty or deth. —CHORUS.

Grasp the sturdy blade of reason,
  Bright from thoughts within;
Cowardice is direst treason,
  Ignorance is sin.
Nature's arsenal is redy,
  Potent is her breth;
Freemen, form then, strong and stedy,
  Liberty or deth. —CHORUS.

Fanny C. Allen.   Adapted by E. B. B.

33. PRESENT SALVATION.

C. M. *Tune—Antioch.*

Salvation, O the joyful sound,
'Tis pleasure to our ears;
A sovereign balm for every wound,
A cordial for our fears.

Salvation from the ills of life,
From fear of deth and hel;
From greed of gain and angry strife,
From passions that rebel.

Salvation, let the echo fly
The spacious earth around;
Til every human soul may cry
Salvation we hav found.

Adapted by E. B. B.

---

34. SEIZE UPON TRUTH.

C. M. *Tune—Arlington.*

ize upon truth where'er 'tis found,
Among your frends or foes,
n Christian or on Heathen ground,
Where'er the blossom grows.

Prove all things; hold to what is good;
The truth shal make you free."
hese ar our doctrins, and we dred
No endles misery.

Only the true free-thinker knows
A perfect peace and rest;
The Christian understands it not,
For anguish fils his brest.

Fear of an endles hel of pain
In store for child or wife,
Or kindred dear, or sinful world,
Poisons his cup of life.

O may the souls of erring men
By truth be rendered free,
And brought into the perfect law
Of Love and Liberty.

Eliza B. Burnz.

---

35.   ROCK OF REASON.

7s *Tune—Toplady.*

Rock of Reason, made for me,
Let me bild my home on thee;
Then when pours the mighty floo(
Showers of water and of blood,
Drawn from superstition's veins,
Firmly stil my home remains.

Blasts of opposition rise,
Threts and thunder fil the skies;
Priestly bulls with awful roar,
Dred anathemas do pour;
Stil my soul can smile serene,
While upon my rock I lean.

Houses bilt upon the sand,
By imagination's hand,
Totter when the clouds of dout,
Pour their angry waters out;
Fall in ruins and destroy,
All who dwel in folly's toy.

E. B. Burnz.

36. THE DAYS AR GOING BY.

P. M. *Tune—Harwell.*

There ar lonely hearts to cherish
  While the days ar going by.
There ar weary souls who perish
  While the days ar going by.
If a smile we can renew,
As our journey we pursue,
O the good we all may do
  While the days ar going by!

There's no time for idle scorning
  While the days ar going by;
Be our faces like the morning,
  While the days ar going by.
O the world is full of sighs,
Full of sad and weeping eyes;
Help your fallen brother rise
  While the days ar going by.

All the loving links that bind us,
  While the days ar going by,
One by one, we leave behind us
  While the days ar going by;

But the seeds of good we sow,
Both in shade and shine wil grow,
And wil keep our hearts aglow
    While the days ar going by.

———

37. PULL FOR THE SHORE.

Light in the darknes, sailor, day is at
    hand ;
See o'er the foaming billows, Fair Haven's
    land.
Drear was the voyage, sailor, now almost
    o'er,
Safe within the life-boat, sailor, pull for the
    shore.
    CHORUS—Pull for the shore, sailor, pull
        for the shore,
        Heed not the rolling waves, but
            bend to the oar ;
        In the life-boat, "Science," sailor,
            cling to "Church" no more,
        Leave the poor old stranded wrecl
            and pull for the shore.

Trust in the life-boat, sailor, all else wil
    fail,
Stronger the surges dash and fiercer the
    gale;
Heed not the stormy winds tho' loudly
    they roar;
Watch the morning star of Truth, and pull
    for the shore. —CHORUS.

Bright gleams the morning, sailor, up lift
    the eye,
Clouds and darknes disappearing, sun-
    shine is nigh ;
Safe in the life-boat, sailor, sing ever-
    more
"Liv for Truth and Reason, boys," and
    pull for the shore. —CHORUS.

        P. P. Bliss—Adapted by E. B. B.

38.   ODE TO SCIENCE.

Tune—New Haven.

My faith looks up to thee,
Light of the living free,
    Science divine ;
Though I nor kneel nor pray,
Thou tak'st my fear away,
O let me from this day
    Be wholly thine.

May thy rich grace impart
Strength to my fainting heart,
    And zeal inspire.
What thou hast given to me
I wil restore to thee—
Thy champion ever be,
    Thy beacon fire.

While life's dark maze I tred,
And sorrows 'round me spred,
    Be thou my guide;

Bid darknes turn to day,
Drive useles griefs away,
Nor let me ever stray
From thee aside.

Channing Burnz.

---

39. WORSHIP OF NATURE.

Tune—Auld Lang Syne.

They tel us that we worship not,
Nor sing sweet songs of praise,
That love divine is not our lot,
In these cold modern days;
That piety's calm peaceful state
We banish from the earth;
They know not that we venerate
Whate'er we see of worth.

The singing of the birds on high,
The rippling of the stream,
The sparkling stars in yon bright sky,
The sunlight's merry gleam,
The ocean's wide and watery main,
The lightning's vivid flash,
The sweet and gentle showers of rain,
The awful thunder's crash;

The trees and flow'rs that deck the land,
The soft and grassy mead,
The firm-set earth on which we stand,
Ar worshipful indeed.

We venerate great Nature's plan,
And worship at her shrine,
While goodnes, truth, and love in man,
We hold to be divine.   *G. Sexton.*

---

40.   WORK.

Work, for the night is coming,
Work through the morning hours;
Work, while the dew is sparkling;
Work 'mid springing flowers;
Work when the day grows brighter,
Work in the glowing sun;
Work, for the night is coming,
When man's work is done.

Work, for the night is coming,
Work through the sunny noon;
Fil brightest hours with labor,
Rest comes sure and soon.
Giv every flying minute
Something to keep in store;
Work for the night is coming,
When man works no more.

Work, for the night is coming,
Under the sunset skies;
While their bright tints ar glowing,
Work, for daylight flies.
Work, til the last beam fadeth,
Fadeth to shine no more;
Work while the night is dark'ning,
When man's work is o'er.   *S. Dyer.*

Sowing the seed by the daylight fair,
Sowing the seed by the noon-day glare,
Sowing the seed by the fading light,
Sowing the seed in the solemn night.
    Oh, what shal the harvest be?

    CHORUS—Sown in the darknes or sown
      in the light,
      Sown in our weaknes or sown in
      our might,
      Gatherd by us or humanity,
      Sure, ah, sure, wil the harvest be.

Sowing the seed by the wayside high,
Sowing the seed on the rocks to die,
Sowing the seed where the thorns wil
    spoil,
Sowing the seed in the fertil soil.
    Oh, what shal the harvest be?

Sowing the seed of a lingering pain,
Sowing the seed of a maddend brain,
Sowing the seed of a tarnisht name,
Sowing the seed of remorse and shame
    Oh, what shal the harvest be?

Sowing the seed with an aching heart,
Sowing the seed while the tear-drop
    start,
Sowing in hope til the reapers come
Redy to gather the harvest home.
    Oh, what shal the harvest be?

      P. P. Bliss—Adapted by E. B. B.

42. THE TIME HAS COME.

8s. Tune—Jesus of Nazareth Passeth By.

The time has come to stand erect
In noble, manly self-respect ;
To see the bright sun over hed,
To feel the ground beneath our tred,
Unled by priests, uncurst by creeds,
Our manhood proving by our deeds.
(Repeat last two lines.)

The time has come to break the yoke,
Whatever cost the needed stroke ;
To set the toiling millions free,
Whatever price their liberty ;
Better a few should die, than all
Be held in worse than deadly thrall.

The time has come for men to find
Their statute-book within the mind ;
To read its laws, and cease to pore
The musty tomes of ages o'er;
Truth's golden rays its page illume,
Her fires your legal scrolls consume.

The time has come to preach the soul ;
No meager-shred, the manly whole ;
Let agitation come, who fears ?
We need a flood ; the filth of years
Has gatherd round us. Roll, then, on;
What cannot stand had best be gone.
Wm. Denton.

43.   NEARER TO TRUTH.

6. 4.   *Tune—Bethany.*

Nearer O Truth to thee,
  Nearer to thee!
E'en though it be a cross
  That raiseth me;
Stil all my song shal be—
‖: Nearer, O Truth, to thee, :‖
  Nearer to thee!

Though like the wanderer,
  The sun gone down,
Darknes be over me,
  My rest a stone:
Yet in my dreams I'd be—
‖: Nearer, O Truth, to thee, :‖
  Nearer to thee!

Then let the way appear
  Steps unto heven;*
All that I suffer here
  In mercy given;
Angels to beckon me
‖: Nearer, O Truth, to thee, :‖
  Nearer to thee!

Or if on fancy's wing,
  Cleaving the sky,
Sun, moon and stars forgot,
  Upward I fly;
Stil all my song shal be,
‖: Nearer O Truth, to thee, :‖
  Nearer to thee!

Sarah F. Adams—Adapted by E. B. B.

---

*NOTE—" Heven" is a condition of supreme satisfaction and enjoyment; a state of mind. "The kingdom of heven is within you, even in your heart," said Jesus.

44. HOMES 'ROUND US HERE.

Tune—Home Over There.

O think of the homes 'round us here,
   Which might all be made joyous and
      bright,
If the world did but see and revere
   One great law, that of justice and
      right.

CHO.—'Round us here, 'round us here,
     O think of the homes 'round us here.

O think of the souls 'round us here,
   Who all homeles life's journey must
      plod,
In despair which refuses a tear;
   Ever robbed in the name of a God.

CHO.—'Round us here, 'round us here,
     The poor homeles souls round us
     here.

Be saviors to these 'round us here;
   And like Jesus denounce and expose,
Evermore without favor or fear,
   The false piety propping our woes.

CHO.—'Round us here, 'round us here,
     Save these from the hels round
     us here.

Could all earnest piety here,
   To our dear fellow mortals be given,
This earth from all sorrow 'twould clear,
   And bring to us the kingdom of heven.

CHO.—'Round us here, 'round us here,
    'Twould soon build a home 'round
      us here. *Caleb S. Weeks—Adapted.*

---

45.   WATCHMAN TEL US.

Watchman! tel us of the night,
   What its signs of promis ar,
Traveler! o'er yon mountain hight,
   See that glory-beaming star.

Watchman! does its beauteous ray
   Aught of hope or joy fortel?
Traveler! yes; it brings the day,
   Promist day of Israel.

Watchman! tel us of the night;
   Higher yet that star ascends.
Traveler! blesednes and light;
   Peace and truth its course portends.

Watchman! wil its beams alone,
   Gild the spot that gave them birth?
Traveler! ages ar its own;
   See it bursts o'er all the earth.

Watchman! tel us of the night,
   For the morning seems to dawn.
Traveler! darknes takes its flight.
   Dout and terror ar withdrawn.

Watchman! joy o'er every land
   Bids us Good, all good adore.
Traveler! join we heart and hand,
   Worship, praise it, evermore.
           J. Bowring—Adapted.

46.   OUR NEEDS.

Tune—I need thee every hour.

We need it every hour,
  A purpose high,
To give us strength and power
  To do or die.

CHORUS—We need it, O we need it,
      Every hour we need it;
      Since coming ages call us
      To aid and guide.

We need it every hour,
  A firm brave wil,
That tho' hate's clouds may lower
  Shal conquer stil. —CHORUS.

We need it every hour
  A calm strong mind,
Enriched by Reason's dower,
  Not warped or blind. —CHORUS.

We need it every hour,
  To use with skil,
Speech to make bigots cower,
  Or hearts to thril. —CHORUS.

We need it every hour
  A patient love,
Which shal all souls endower
  From hights above. —CHORUS.

We need it every hour
A conscience clear,
That shal be as a tower
Of strength and cheer.   —CHORUS

We need it every hour,
A true pure life,
Which failure cannot sour
Or turn to strife.   —CHORUS.

Sara A. Underwood.

47.   LOVE DIVINE.

8, 7, *Tune—Violet.*

Love Divine, all love impeling,
Joy of heven, to earth come down,
Evermore within us dweling,
All our lives with wisdom crown.
Father, Mother! —vital spirit,
Love's unbounded life thou art;
Let us more thy love inherit;
Fil to fullnes every heart.!

Let, O let life's richest tresure
Overflow from every brest,
Filling earth with hevenly plesure,
Giving souls divinest rest.
Come, almighty to deliver!
Strife and darknes then wil flee,
And the earth, matured, shal ever
Yield the fruits of harmony!

Caleb S. Weeks.

48. THE GLORIOUS BAND.

C. M. *Tune—Warwick.*

A holy spirit goes to war,
 To break the captive's chain;
A snow white banner shows afar—
 Who follows in that train?

Who best can drain the cup of woe
 And triumf over pain;
Who patient bear both stripe and blow,
 He follows in the train.

The martyr, he whose eagle eye
 Could pierce beyond the grave,
Who like his master, fain would die,
 Where deth men's souls could save.

The men of thought, Truth's chosen few,
 On whom her spirit came;
Who studied, suffered, died, stil true
 To that most bleséd name.

They've climbed the dizzy steep of heven
 Through scorn and toil and shame;
They've dived thro' hel, and knowledge
 given,
 To save men from its pain.

O praise to Faith and Charity
 And Hope, sweet sisters three!
And praise, beyond all parity,
 O Science unto thee.

 Channing Burnz.

49.   BLOW YE THE TRUMPET.

H. M.   *Tune—Lenox.*

Blow ye the trumpet, blow
  With loud exulting sound ;
Let all the nations know
  To earth's remotest bound,
The year of jubilee has come;
Return, ye wanderers, return !

Ye slaves of dogma-creeds
  And superstition's fright,
Now, answering your needs,
  See ! Nature sends her light.
The year of juiblee has come ;
Return to freedom's light, return !

Ye who from priestlings think
  To gain a hevenly day,
See ! from their creeds they shrink
  Explaining them away,
The year of jubilee has come;
Return to Nature's light, return !
                                   Caleb S. Weeks.

---

50.   NATURE'S TRUMPET.

C. M.   *Tune—Brown.*

Let every human ear attend,
  And every heart rejoice,
For Nature's gospel-trumpet sounds
  With an inviting voice.

Ho, all ye hungry, starving souls
Who feed upon the wind;
Who with tradition's dogma-toys,
Would fil an empty mind;

Eternal wisdom here prepares
A soul supplying feast,
And bids your longing appetites
The rich provision taste.

Ho, ye that pant for living streams,
And pine away and die,
Here you may quench your raging thirst
With springs that never dry.

The gates of Nature's gospel grace
Stand open night and day;
Here all may find complete supplies,
And drive their wants away.
Caleb S. Weeks.

---

51.   LIGHT OF THE WORLD.

C. M.   *Tune—Antioch.*

Joy to the world! the light is come;
The only lawful king;
Let every heart prepare it room,
And moral nature sing.

Joy to the earth! now Reason reigns;
Let men their songs employ;
While fields and floods, rocks, hils, and
plains,
Repeat the sounding joy.

No more let superstition grow,
  Nor thorns infest the ground;
This light wil make its blesings flow
  To earth's remotest bound.

O, then display its truth and peace,
  And make the nations prove
The glories of its tendernes,
  The wonders of its love.

---

52. ALL HAIL, THE TRUTH.

C. M.   *Tune—Coronation.*

All hail the Truth! behold, he comes!
  See, errors prostrate fall!
He comes with royal diadem,
  And crowned the Lord of all!

He comes to all—no chosen race
  No partial remnant small;
He givs to all his soverign grace;
  He comes the Lord of all!

Let every kindred, every tribe
  On this terrestrial ball,
To him all majesty ascribe,
  And crown him Lord of all!

Then with the mighty, joyous throng
  Arising from their thrall,
We'l join in an exulting song
  To Truth—the Lord of all!

Adapted by Caleb S Weeks

53. STAR OF TRUTH.

8, 7, 4. *Tune—Rousseau's Dream.*

(*Also known as* " *Greenville.*")

Guide us, Truth, thou star refulgent!
Trav'lers through a darksome land;
We ar weak, but thou art mighty
To support our social band;
Lead us onward,
Answering to thy high command.

Open, now, the crystal fountains,
Whence thy healing waters flow;
Bathe us and refresh our spirits,
As we on our journey go,
Blis expecting,
Til we all its plesures know.

When we view thy hev'nly mansion,
Breaking on our aching sight,
Then our fears begin to vanish;
We ar filled with sweet delight;
Joys for ever
Rising to the greatest height.

Safe within, no more we wander;
Here we dwel in peace secure;
Sordid cares no more can tempt us,
Foolish charms no more allure;
Everlasting,
Reason's plesures wil endure.

54. MEMORY OF VOLTAIRE.

7, 6.   Tune—Missionary Hymn.

Hurrah ! the day is breaking,
    The day is breaking fast;
From fevered dreams of ages
    The world has waked at last.
Lo! Freedom shakes the darknes
    With anthem and with lyre,
And bigotry is dying
    Beside her martyr fire!

The world is up and doing,
    Determined to atone
For blood and gloom that circled
    The altar and the throne;
And kingcraft with its demons
    Of flame and gore and lust,
The mitre and the priesthood
    Ar trampled in the dust.

Old Superstition's specters,
    Ar back to chaos hurl'd,
The full sun-burst of knowledge
    Streams o'er the waking world;
And 'mong the sacred relics
    Of noble, true, and fair,
The hearts of men shal cherish
    The memory of Voltaire.

Adapted by E. B. B.

55. HOLD THE FLAG.

Tune—Hold the Fort.

Hark, the trump of Freedom ringing,
  Through the battle's crash!
Let your joyous shout of " Forward !"
  Redy answer flash.
CHORUS—Hold the flag of Freedom flying,
      Through the trubled night;
     Round the crimson banner rally,
      Children of the light !

Boldly follow where she guideth,
  Ever take her part;
Goddes of your worship is she,
  Monarch of your heart.
    CHORUS.

Be your daily work an offering
  Laid upon her shrine;
Never let her blush to own you,
  Make your life sublime.
    CHORUS.

Be your heart a holy altar
  Lit with living flame,
Aspiration's incense rising
  To her sacred name.
    CHORUS.

Gladly to her glorious service
  Dedicate each breth;
If you cannot win her living,
  Conquer her by deth.
    CHORUS.   *Annie Besant.*

56. LIV NOBLY.

Tune— There is a Happy Land.

While on this earth ye stay,
  O, nobly liv;
Strive ye from day to day,
  Some joy to giv,
Some hopeful word to speak,
Fresh strength to giv the weak,
By constant effort seek
  Nobly to liv.

Turn ye with generous heart
  Toward those who need—
Eager to sow some part
  Of life's good seed.
Forego mere selfish gains ;
Think ye of others claims ;
Make e'en your simplest aims
  Noble indeed.

Listen to conscience' voice,
  Thy surest guide ;
Its teachings make thy choice,
  By them abide ;
Walk ye with earnest feet,
Holding all duty meet ;
So shal contentment sweet
  Walk by thy side.

And when the end draws near,
  The dreamles rest,
All labor finished here,
  Ended all quest,

Calmly turn ye to sleep,
Though loving hearts shal weep;
Immortal they shal keep
   Thy noblest—best.   *C. Godfrey.*

---

57.   AWAKE! ARISE!

H. M.   *Tune—Lenox.*

Hark! through the waking earth,
  Hark! through the echoing sky,
Herald of freedom's birth,
  There comes a glorious cry—
    Awake! arise! The day's at hand;
    For Truth and Freedom take your stand.

The triple chains that bind,
  Fall from the weary limb,
Fall from the down-crushed mind,
  As rolls that noble hymn.
    Awake! arise! etc.

Unto man's waiting heart
  It saith, "Arise, be strong!
Bear thou an earnest part
  Against all forms of wrong."
    Awake. arise, etc.

"Bid fear giv place to love;
  Bid crime and passion cease;
Be every word of hate
  Forever husht in peace"
    Awake! arise! etc.
             Adapted by E. B. B.

58.   RISE, MY SOUL.

P. M.   *Tune—Amsterdam.*

Rise my soul expand thy wings,
  Thine only portion trace ;
Rise from superstitious things,
  To truth, thy native place;
Sun and moon and stars remain,
Changing ever as they move ;
Rise, my soul, thy portion claim,
  In Nature's equal love.

Cease, sad spirit, cease thy strife,
  Nor murmer at thy clime ;
Liv a happy, virtuous life,
  And taste the joys of time;
'Midst thy friends and kindred dwel,
Take what truth and nature send,
Cheerful bid the world farewel,
  Whene'er thy life shal end.

Abner Kneeland.

59.   REIGN OF FREEDOM.

C. M.   *Tune—St. Martin's.*

Behold, the reign of Freedom comes !
  That reign expected long ;
Let ev'ry heart exult with joy,
  And ev'ry voice be song.

It comes the pris'ners to relieve,
  In slavery's bondage held :

The gates of brass before it burst,
  The iron fetters yield.

It comes from clouds of ignorance
  To clear the inward sight,
And on the opening powers of mind
  To pour instructive light.

Our voices in triumfant song
  Thy welcome shal proclaim,
And spred to all the earth abroad
  The honors .of thy name.

---

60.   MAN OF REASON.

C. M. D.   *Tune—Brattle Street.*

Up, Man of reason, rouse thee up !
  This is no slumbering age ;
Begird thyself, unbare thy arm,
  And for the right engage.
Stern duty's voice demands thine help,
  Arouse the for the strife,
Be up and doing—for the world
  With mighty change is rife.

Already much has been achievd,
  There's much more to be done ;
But aid the work with all your strength,
  The good shal yet be won.
O'erleap the barriers prejudice
  May set across your way ;
Hope on—take courage—persevere,
  And yours shal be the day.

61.   LIBERAL HYMN.

6. 4.   *Tune—America.*

Humanity, for thee,
And for thy liberty,
  Our legions plead !
Now be each tyrant's chain,
Forever broke in twain ;
Our work prove not in vain,
  For thine and thee.

O brothers ! unto ye,
Who would be nobly free,
  In love we come ;
And in the name of right,
And Freedom's holy light,
Abjure and spurn the blight
  Of priestly craft.

An altar new, to thee   .
We raise, O Liberty ;
  Our incense burn.
The old things past away,
New things ris'n from decay
Shal crown with deathles lay
  Our righteous cause.

Reason, we cry to thee,
Author of Liberty,
  To bles this day !
Let truth and love prevail,
Nor strength nor curage fail,
Till we the days shal hail
  When thought is free !
                    Mrs. J. B. Brown.

62. TRUTH SEEKERS.

S. M. *Tune—Silver Street.*

For truth where wil ye seek?
    Where find its place of birth?
Think ye 'twas born on Sinai's peak,
    There given to the earth?

Think ye its endles fire,
    Flamed first on Hebrew page,
Think ye it could alone inspire,
    Priests of a bygone age?

Hath it no record true,
    Save in the ancient time?
Could no one but a pagan jew,
    Receive the word sublime?

Was God asleep til then?
    And through th' eternal years,
Could nothing but a Hebrew pen
    Record the birth of years?

Nay, back beyond their ken,
    Beyond what legends taught,
This grand old earth gave birth to men
    Whose lives were filled with thought.

They sought and found the truth,
    'Tis written everywhere,
Its record true, is red by youth
    In earth and viewles air.

Each soul can light its fires,
    We need no priestly line;

The more our souls to truth aspire,
    The more on us 'twil shine.
Horace M. Richards,—Adapted by E. B. B.

---

63.   KIND WORDS.

Tune—Last Rose of Summer.

What a world of deep sweetnes
    There is in the tone,
That comes to us kindly
    When weary and lone:
Enwreathd with the laurel,
    What rest could we find,
If love never cheerd us
    With words that ar kind?

The floating of music,
    When morning is bright,
May fall on the spirit
    Like droppings of light.
For O, they ar plesant—
    The hymns of the birds;
But never, no never,
    So sweet as kind words.

I've sat in the shadow
    Of twilight's soft wing,
And dreamd about angels
    And songs that they sing;
They'r lovely—such visions
    By fancy combined,
But O, how much sweeter
    Ar words that ar kind.

64. TO GRUMBLERS.

8. 7. *Tune—Yankee Doodle.*

'Tis true the world is very bad,
　No mortal soul can blink it;
But then 'tis not so dedly vile
　As some fault-finders think it.

CHO.—As some fault-finders think it, sir,
　　As some fault-finders think it;
　But then 'tis not so dedly vile
　　As some fault-finders think it.

No dout, dark shadows cross the earth,
　Scarce liven'd by a stray light;
But how is it, these shades ar seen?
　We liv in virtue's daylight.

CHO.—We liv in virtue's daylight, sir,
　　We liv in virtue's daylight;
　That's how it is these shades ar seen,
　　We liv in virtue's daylight.

The deeds at which our fathers smiled,
　Nor thought a man the worse for,
We look upon with deep disgust,
　And giv our direst curse for.

CHO.—And giv our direst curse, etc.

The world is but a school-boy yet,
　Its daily lesson learning;
Its teacher, life, to make it wise,
　New pages ever turning.

CHO.—New pages ever turning. etc.

Then cease this everlasting growl,
  Be gentle, kind, and tender ;
And since the world is bad, let's join
  And do our best to mend her.

CHO.—And do our best to mend, etc.

Wm. Denton.

65, THE WORLD IS GROWING BETTER.

Tune—Yankee Doodle.

Hear ye the cry, O men of earth ?
  O'er sea and land 'tis sounding ;
Old formulas ar breaking up
  And new-born hopes ar bounding.
The dawn of day has struck away
  From tawny slave his fetter,
O happy hour, O glorious time,—
  The world is growing better !

'Tis said the world is growing old,
  'Tis rather growing youthful—
Old fogyism melts away
  Before a wisdom truthful.
If Ignorance stil frown and scold
  At coming times, why let her,
Mankind no more shal own her sway,
  The world is growing better !

Lita Barney Sayles.

Songs of Progres,

66 THE DAY BREAKETH.

L. M. *Tune—Old Hundred.*

The records of the olden time
Giv place to truths far more sublime;
The mists and darknes fade away
Before the light of dawning day.

Truth's mighty power o'er all the land
Wil break old Superstition's band,
Til not an error shal remain
To fetter human souls again.

Truth's mighty flow is ocean wide,
Its power as great as ocean's tide;
Resistles as the march of time,
Its tidal wave so grand, sublime—

Shal sweep old errors from its path,
And for the old time God of wrath
Shal open wide the doors above,
And show us all that God is love.

H. M. Richards.

67. TO SCIENCE. 6, 6, 4.

Glad voices let us raise,
And sing triumfant praise
This day to see;

For on our mental sight,
Now rising in its might,
Beams Science, glorious light,
Mankind to free.

All o'er our favored land
Old ignorance we command,
Our presence leave;
Truth, without church or state,
Be ours to consecrate ;
And by it, victory great
We wil achieve.

J. H. Cook.

---

68.   BRIGHTER DAY.

8, 6.   *Tune—Auld Lang Syne.*

O bright the day that dawneth now,
And brighter stil shal be,
When gloom wil vanish from our brow,
And trammeled thought be free;
When truth shal gild our mental sky,
And errors fade away—
Sure, science fair most fervently
Proclaims the coming day.

When slaves no more shal walk the
earth,
Nor tyrants rule the hour,
When man shal rise to greater worth
In majesty and power ;
And Nature's laws, as good supreme,
Shal all his acts control,
And virtue with its brightest beam
Shal harmonize his soul.

Then let our hearts in joyous strain
  Sing loudest notes of praise,
And worship Truth,—be this our aim,—
  In whatsoever fase ;
In deepest cave or hevens high,
  In science or in art,
Its treasures bright let none decry,
  But cherish in the heart.

Mrs. Sophie W. Kent.

——————

69. STAR OF PROGRES. 8, 7.

Star of Progres, guide us onward,
  By thy ever glorious light,
May our motto e'er be—"Onward,"
  Swerve not to the left nor right.

O illume our souls when sorrow
  Gathers clouds around our hearts;
Show to us the joyous morrow
  Which but life and joy imparts.

O we greet thy beams with gladnes,—
  Promis of a brighter day,
Which shal chase away all sadnes,
  While bright glories round us play.

Shine thou on, thou starry token
  Of the joys that ar to come,
When with love's bright chain unbroken,
  We shal all be gathered home.

70. ETERNAL PROGRES.

Tune—Auld Lang Syne.

Come, let us join in cheerful song,
  With hope's inspiring lay;
With praise prolongd, let every tongue
  Proclaim this joyful day;
For truth immortal rends the veil
  Of error's dark domain,
And every gloomy fantom fades
  At reason's glorious reign.

The earth and sky ar all aglow
  With orbs of living light,
While truth's victorious banners rise
  On every mountain hight,
Take curage, then, O douting soul;
  For all that's great and good
Wil be revealed to every mind,
  As truth is understood.

No sin-atoning sacrifice
  Can banish pain and woe;
But manfully we learn to liv
  By reaping what we sow;
The bitter fruits of each misdeed
  As kindly point the way,
As do the joys in sweet return,
  When truth we most obey.

Eternal progres marks the path
  Of each immortal soul,
And though in weaknes we may fall,
  We rise to self-control;

Thus right wil over wrong prevail,
 If truth be understood,
For wickednes shal not avail
 To crush eternal good.

W. S. Barlow.

---

71. A NEW FAITH. C. M.

Let superstition be destroyd
 And falshood cast away,
That liberty may be enjoyd,
 And truth hold sov'reign sway.

Let thought be free to all mankind,
 And reason's light illume
The long-benighted relms of mind,
 Dispeling clouds of gloom.

Let conscience rule us every day,
 That we may honor truth,
And her supreme commands obey
 Through life, from early youth.

Let kindnes fil the human heart
 With sympathy for all,
And bid us knowledge to impart,
 The mind to disenthrall.

Let love prevail in every brest,
 And happines abound;
May all mankind be truly blest,—
 Humanity be crown'd.

72. THE BETTER CHOICE. L. M.

Ah! wretched minds, who stil remain
    Mere slaves to superstition's din!
A nobler toil may I sustain,
    A nobler satisfaction win.

I would resolve with all my heart,
    With all my powers true peace pursue;
Nor from these precepts e'er depart,
    Which hav the good of man in view.

O, be this service all my joy,
    Around let my example shine,
Til others love the blest employ,
    And join in labors so sublime.

Be this the purpose of my heart,
    My solemn, my determined choice,
To ever act the virtuous part,
    And in the ways of truth rejoice.

---

73. THE WORLD MOVES.

8. 7. *Tune—Sicily.*

O, the world is moving onward,
    With a grand resistles tred,
While the anthems of the living
    Drown th' requiems for the ded.

Yes! Humanity is waking
    From old error's gloomy night;

Christian forms and shams ar breaking,
  While the cause of truth grows bright.

Mind and matter ever blending,
  In the human form divine,
Giv us trust in life unending,
  That must christian hopes outshine.

---

74. FRUITS OF CONCORD. L. M.

Happy the land of every clime,
  Where Science beams her lucid rays;
Where nativ truths with luster shine,
  Attuning every heart to praise.

Where fairest fruits of knowledge grow,
  And wisdom doth her charms display,
Where tears of sorrow cease to flow,
  Or kindnes wipes them all away.

The vernal songster's tuneful notes,
  To honest labor all invite;
The fields and gardens yield their fruits,
  The husbandman they thus requite.

But discord poisons human blis,—
  To plesure is a dedly foe;
It fils the mind with deep distres,
  And sinks the heart to bitter woe.

Then let us all in union join,
  And ever seek the common weal;
Let love and charity combine,
  Each other's errors all to heal.

75. THE BEAUTIES OF NATURE.

8, 7.   *Tune—Nettleton.*

Look around the fields of Nature,
   Plesant scenes, how richly gay;
What a home for ev'ry creature,
   Doth the universe display!
See the earth with air surrounded,
   Ocean, with her deep profound;
All with life and stir abounding,
   Happy millions all around.

Then we'l praise all bounteous Nature;
   Praise shal flow from ev'ry tongue;
Let us join with ev'ry creature,
   Join the universal song;
For the hours of social plesure,
   For the hope of future days,
For th' extent of life's full mesure,
   Shout aloud all Nature's praise.

Abner Kneeland.

76. LAWS OF NATURE. C. M.

The laws of Nature they ar sure,
   They make the simple wise;
That man mistakes his safest guide
   Who does those laws despise.

The statutes of those laws ar right,
   And wil improve the heart;
To all who follow where they lead
   They health and joy impart.

Because they teach the sons of men,
How they their lives should frame:
A rich reward they wil bestow
On all who keep the same.

---

77. LEARN OF NATURE. 8, 7.

Nature is the safest teacher
For the darkend mind of man;
Listen to this ancient preacher
As the wisest in the land.

Nature's laws in mind and body,
Nature's laws in earth and sky
Wil reveal to all their duty
And the bigot's frown defy.

Sacred books and man-made bibles,
Musty with the mold of time,
Made by barbarous popes and councils,
Ar not guides to truths sublime.

Working through all forms and forces
Love and wisdom guide the whole;
Listen to their sacred voices,
As inspirers of the soul.

Nature's laws ar laws unchanging,
Sweeping through the cosmos wide;
Dealing sorrow to us, erring,
Blis, if we those laws abide.

D. Higbie—adapted.

78.   THE WORLD IS YOUNG.

7. 6.   Tune—Webb.

The world is young, my brothers;
   We're all here in good time.
Cease groaning, foolish preacher,
   The earth is in her prime.

When did the sun shine brighter?
   Who saw the moon more fair?
Who knows Spring's breth more balmy?
   More sweet the fragrant air?

Stil sing the flowing rivers,
   Stil chant the rolling seas;
And anthems rise to heven
   From budding forest trees.

In Nature's face no wrinkle;
   Care writes not on her brow;
When "sang the stars of morning,"
   Les fair was she than now.

Stil livs the tree of freedom,
   Whose boughs bear fruit for all,
And poison for the tyrant
   Who would a soul enthrall.

We'l sing the old world young then,
   With beauty on its brow;
This globe was never fairer,
   In bygone days than now. -- *Wm. Denton.*

79. THE PLACE OF WORSHIP.

L. M. *Tune—Hebron.*

The place of worship is not bound
  By archéd roofs and stone-bilt walls,
Where prayers ar said in weary round,
  As custom leads or church bel calls.

Where solem forms the truth encrust,
  The real hides beneath pretense ;
And ages of tradition's dust
  Stil blind and choke the moral sense.

In flowery fields with bees and birds,
  The heart may leap and join their hymn;
Worship is not confined to words
  In gloomy cells and cloisters dim.

'Tis where the hand with nature vies,
  And, ever working, blessing brings ;
'Tis where the mind with reverence tries
  To find the mysteries of things.

The joyful heart is highest praise,
  Work, thought, and love, the loftiest
      prayer ;
These consecrate all times and days,
  And bid the soul to worship there.
                              F. Barrington.

80. HIGHER GROUND. C. M.

Through relms of earnest, lofty thought,
　Which seers and sages knew,
I seek the Trine that Plato sought,
　The Lovely, Good and True.

I greet the silence deep and grand,
　The solitude profound,
The mystic, breezy Upper-Land
　With peace and beauty crownd.

Beneath—the war of angry sects,
　The clash of hostil creeds ;
Above—the joy that love perfects,
　The rest that strife succeeds.

Up, heart! and seek the shining rays
　That flood the azure height—
The mountain-tops and golden days,
　Freedom and Strength and Light!

---

81. TO REASON.

S. M. Tune—Shirland.

O Reason ! full of grace,
　With a glad heart and free,
Myself, my residue of days,
　I consecrate to thee.

Thy willing servant, I
　Restore to thee thine own ;
And from this moment, liv or die,
　I serve but thee alone.

Elmina D. Slenker.

82. RISE, REASON. C. M.

Rise, Reason, shine on all our race,
  Shed confidence around;
For where thou guid'st our wand'ring
    steps
  Is sure, is solid ground.

Rise, sun that lights the mental world,
  And drive night's visions hence;
Dispel the cloud of error's gloom
With beams of common sense.

Shine, from the eastern shore to west;
  Extend from sea to sea;
Til all the nations of the earth
Illuminated be.

The day wil come; the happy day
  Is spreding o'er the sky,
When truth shal chase vain dreams away,
  And midnight fantoms fly.

---

83. REASON. C. M.

Reason, the frend of human kind,
  Long banisht from her throne,
Has burst the veil of gloomy night,
  And claims us as her own.

O what a night was that which wrapt
  The human mind in gloom!
O what a sun which breaks this day
  On superstition's doom!

Ten thousand happy voices join
  To hail the glorious morn;
'Twil scatter blessings far and wide,
  To nations yet unborn.

----

84.   A BRIGHTER DAY.

Comrades! see o'er yonder hil tops
  Gleams of light appear;
Brighter, stronger, clearer growing,
  Day wil soon be here.
Cho.—Faithful be to Reason's standard,
     Fear not Error's powers;
    Truth is strong and sure to conquer,
     Vict'ry must be ours.

Not the light from pious altars,
  Red with scenes of deth,
But the light of Reason breaking
  Through the gloom of faith.
Cho.—Faithful be, etc.

Long the night of superstition
  Wrapped the earth with gloom;
Now the glorious rays of reason
  Shal her vales illume.
Cho—Faithful be etc.

Slowly, surely, brightly, grandly,
  Spreds the glorious light,
Harbinger of all that's precious,
  Freedom, Truth, and Right.
Cho.—Faithful be, etc.

Chas. Stephenson.

85. WHAT WE WANT. C. M.

We want no counsel from the priest,
  No bishop's crook or gown,
No sanctimonious righteousnes,
  No curse or godly frown.

We want no Bibles in the school,
  No creeds or doctrins there,
We want no superstition's tool
  The children's mind to scare.

We want the rights of Liberty,
  With Reason's lamp to try
Each word and thought of other men,
  To solv our destiny.

We want the wrongs of life to hav,
  A cure that's felt to-day,—
A savior, not beyond the grave,—
  To work, and not to pray.

We want to reverence the right
  That's felt and understood,
And not with Superstition's blight,
  To fear an angry God.

We want our paradise on earth—
  Not saints, but honest men,
Whose lives shal need no second birth,
  Or Savior rudely slain.

And having these, the work shal grow;
  Each effort shal set free
A thinking man, whose voice shal go
  To shout for liberty.

86. ODE TO SUPERSTITION.

Tune—Bruce's Address.

Scurge and tyrant of the land,
Kindler of dissension's brand,
Drop from out thy palsied hand,
   Th' septer of thy sway !

We hav burst thy hated chain—
We disown thy blighting reign,
Ne'er wil we be slaves again,
   Reason points our way.

Superstition bows her hed—
Falsehood sleeps among the ded,
Bigotry's exulting tred,
   Now cannot condem.

Sal'ried sons may mourn her fall—
Pastors to their flocks may call;
They no more our minds enthrall;
   Reason cries—Amen.

87. FREEDOM'S CHARMS.

7s. Tune—Hendon.

Freedom's charms alike engage
Blooming youth and hoary age;
None ar happy but the free;
Blis is born of liberty.

Though all other joys were mine,
'Midst those joys I should repine,

If my strong and valiant soul
Felt the harshnes of control.

For one day with freedom spent
Yieldeth more sincere content,
Than a whole eternal round
In the chains of slav'ry bound.

Giv me freedom while I liv,
For my guide, pure wisdom giv,
Giv me goodnes for my frend,
Happines wil then attend.

---

88. DEEDS, NOT WORDS.

L. M. *Tune—Uxbridge.*

Bound fast to creed, who can be free,
And feel the joys of Liberty?
He is in thraldom of the soul
Whose life both church and creed control.

For to be free, aye, free indeed.
One must throw off the chains of creed,
And let the soul untrammeld soar,
Free as the winds forevermore,

To read the laws of life and love,
In rolling earth—the worlds above;
For Nature's face unerring givs
A "Holy writ" that ever lives.

No records of the misty lore,
Can teach me what I must adore;

No worded revelation given,
Can point my soul the way to heven.

For as upon this rock I stand,
I read God's Scriptures plowd in land;
When night comes on with worlds outspred,
I read them on that radient bed.

And when my soul looks up to thee,
Thou endles space, Infinity,
I humbly bow, for God has given
Yon burning worlds to light to heven.

                                R. Lapham.

-----

89.   NOBLE LIVES. 8. 7.

There ar hearts that never falter
  In the battle for the right;
There ar ranks that never alter
  Watching through the darkest night.
And the agony of sharing
  In the fiercest of the strife,
Only givs a nobler daring,
  Only makes a grander life.

There ar those who never weary,
  Bearing suffering and wrong;
Though the way is long and dreary,
  It is vocal with their song.
While their spirits in Truth's furnace,
  Bending to its gracious wil,
Ar becoming purer, fairer,
  By its loving matchles skil.

There ar those whose loving mission
  Is to bind the bleeding heart,

And to teach the calm submission
  Where the pain and sorrow smart;
They ar angels bearing to us,
  Love's rich ministry of peace,
When the night is nearing to us,
  And life's bitter trials cease.

There ar those who battle slander,
  Envy, hatred and all wrong,
Who would rather die than pander
  To the passions of the strong ;
And no earthly power can crush them,
  They ar conquerors of fate ;
Neither fear nor favor crush them,---
  These alone ar truly great.

---

90. FREEDOM'S STRENGTH. C. M.

I'd rather wear a crown of thorns,
  With souls who dare be free,
Than own the costliest diadem
  At price of liberty.

Let folly scof, and cowards creep,
  The strong must walk alone ;
There's secret joy in freedom's strength,
  The weak hav never known.

The valiant-hearted fear no storms
  That beat 'gainst freedom's side ;
Nor shrink before the foeman's steel—
  Scars ar the hero's pride.

Jennie H. Foster.

91.   BE THYSELF.

8. 7.   Tune—Autumn.

Be thyself; a nobler gospel
    Never preached the Nazarene.
Be thyself; 'tis holy scripture,
    Though no Bible lids between.

Dare to shape the thought in language
    That is lying in thy brain;
Dare to launch it, banners flying,
    On the bosom of the main.

Be no parrot, idly prating
    Thoughts the spirit never knew;
Be a profet of the God-sent,
    Telling all thy message true.

Then tho' coward world may scorn thee,
    Frendship fail and fortune frown.
Heven itself grow dark above thee,
    Gods in anger thence look down;

Heed not; there's a world more potent
    Carried in thy manly heart.
Be thyself and do thy duty;
    It wil always take thy part.

If the God within says, "Wel done,"
    What ar other gods to thee?
Hel's his frown; but, where his smile is,
    There is heven for the free.

             Wm. Denton.—Adapted.

92.   TRUST THYSELF.

8. 7. Tune—Sicily.

Trust thyself! believe, endevor,
  Try again, though hope should fail;
Hope is mortal; Faith for ever
  Liveth—living must prevail.

Trust thy fellows! work together,
  E'en the sun works not alone;
Whirling through the width of ether
  Other suns their courses run.

Trust in Truth! she is eternal;
  Let thy wil but fix its root;
Trust in Truth, who in one kernel
  Hideth centuries of fruit.

---

93.   STAND FIRM.   C. M.

Stil firm in purpose ever be
  Wherever drifts the tide,
And bear in mind, whate'er we see,
  The world to all is wide.

O heart, hold fast, though hard it be
  At first to win the way;
The darkest morning in the end
  May prove the brightest day.

As weak a boat has reacht the port
  In spite of every tide;
Fear not that every course wil fail
  Until the whole ar tried.

                    C. G. Leland.

94. TAKE THE HELM. 8, 7.

Be thyself ! There's nothing grander
  Written in thy inmost soul!
Trust thyself and stand the firmest,
  When life's surges wildest roll!

Let thy Reason be thy helmsman,
  He wil guide thy bark aright,
And thy polar star be duty;
  No clouds ever dim that light.

Thou must sail like all around thee,
  Oft in calm and oft in storm;
Oft shalt hear the cordage creaking,
  Oft torn sails come rattling down.

Oft the reefs wil rise before thee,
  Turn thee from thy chosen path;
Overboard shal go thy treasure;
  Oft the past grins like a wraith.

Courage stil ! the storm when ended
  Leaves a smooth and placid sea;
And in place of sails thus rended,
  Stronger sails there then wil be.

In the sted of sunken tresure,
  Richer cargo shalt thou find;
And thy path now seeming wayward,
  Shal prove straight as path of wind.

And the wraith that came to daunt thee
  Then wil prove an angel guide,
That with smile shal beckon onward,
  Into heven's calmer tide.

95. WHAT OF THY LIFE? C. M.

What of thy life, O frend of mine?
  I wil not ask thy creed,
Or whether plant of grace divine
  In thy heart scatters seed.

The form of faith that fils thy want
  I do not care to know;
Nor whether at baptismal font
  Christ's love to thee did flow.

How oft it is you fast and pray
  Alone on bended knee,
Or by what chart you shape your way,
  You need not tel to me.

But tel me if the inborn good
  Stands forth in bold relief;
If virtue ne'er misunderstood,
  Of jewels all, is chief.

And dost thou own from hour to hour,
  Truth's ministrations sweet;
And does her matchles living power
  Make all thy life complete?

Ar all thy days so thickly strewn
  With pure and loving deeds,
That, making others' cares thine own,
  Thou hast forgot *thy* needs?

In all thy ways, hast thou e'er done
  The best thy hand could do?
If so, I'm sure thy crown is won,—
  Fadeles, and pure, and true.

96.   WHAT I LIV FOR.

Tune—Missionary Hymn.

I liv for those who love me,
   For those I know ar true,
For heven that smiles above me,
   And earth so fair to view;
For human ties that bind me,
For tasks by God assigned me,
For bright hopes left behind me,
   And good that I can do.

I liv to learn their story,
   Who suffered for my sake,—
To emulate their glory,
   And follow in their wake;
Bards, patriots, martyrs, sages,
The noble of all ages,
Whose deeds crowd history's pages,
   And time's great volume make.

I liv to hold communion
   With all that is divine;
To feel there is a union
   'Twixt nature's heart and mine;
To profit by affliction,
Reap truths from fields of fiction,
Grow wiser by conviction.
   And fil each grand design.

I liv to hail the season
   By gifted minds foretold,
When men shal rule by reason,
   And not alone by gold;

When man to man united,
And every wrong thing righted,
The whole world shal bo lighted,
By loving joy untold.

---

97. FAITH IN ONE ANOTHER. 8, 7.

Cherish faith in one another,
  When you meet in friendship's name;
In the true frend is a brother,
  And his heart should throb the same.

Though your paths in life may differ,
  Since the hour when first ye met;
Stil hav faith in one another,
  You may need that friendship yet.

O hav faith in one another,
  When ye speak a brother's vow;
It may not be always summer—
  Not be always bright as now.

And when wintry clouds ar hevy,
  If some kindred heart you share,
And hav faith in one another,
  O ye never shal despair.

Then hav faith in one another,
  And let honor be your guide;
Let the truth alone be spoken,
  Whatsoever may betide.

Tho' the false may reign a season,—
  Dout ye not it sometims wil;
Yet hav faith in one another,
  And the truth shal triumf stil.

98.   PERSEVERANCE.

8, 7.   *Tune—Wilmot.*

Take the spade of perseverance;
  Dig the fields of progres wide;
Every rotten root of faction
  Hurry out and cast aside.

Every stubborn root of error,
  Every weed that hurts the soil,
Tares, whose very growth is terror,
  Dig them out, whate'er the toil.

Giv the stream of education
  Broader channel, bolder force;
Hurl the stones of persecution
  Out, where'er they block its course.

Seek for strength in self-exertion;
  Work, and stil hav faith to wait;
Close the crooked gate to fortune,
  Make the path to honor straight.

Men ar agents for the future!
  As they work, so ages win
Either harvest of advancment,
  Or the product of their sin!

Follow out true cultivation,
  Widen education's plan;
From the majesty of Nature
  Teach the majesty of man!

99.   REAL SAVIORS. L. M.

When worth and genius ar combined
In men of heart and activ mind,
And from their noble musings flow
Benignest balm for human woe;

O let us hail the light they giv,
And aid the cause for which they liv,
And grateful twine around their name
The wreath of an undying fame.

Such men ar gems of priceles worth,
The real saviors of the earth;
They bring reforms and show the way
To better things—a brighter day.

                                 W. Camsel.

---

100. WHOM TO HONOR. C, M.

Honor to him who freely gives
    As fortune fils his store;
Who shares the gifts that he receives
    With those who need them more;
Whose melting heart of pity moves
    O'er sorrow and distres;
Of all his friends, who mostly loves
    The poor and fatherles.

Honor to him who shuns to do
    An action mean or low;
Who wil a noble course pursue
    To stranger, frend, or foe;
Who seeks for justice more than gain,
    Is merciful and kind;

Who wil not cause a needles pain
  In body or in mind.

Honor to him who scorns to be
  To name or sect a slave ;
Whose soul is like the sunshine, free,
  Free as the ocean wave ;
Who when he sees oppression, wrong,
  Speaks out in thunder-tones ;
Who feels that he, with truth, is strong
  To grapple e'en with thrones.

———

101.   BRAVE REFORMERS. C. M.

O brave Reformers, not in vain,
  You trust in human kind ;
That good which bloodshed cannot gain,
  Your peaceful zeal shal find.

The truths you urge ar borne abroad
  By every wind and tide ;
The voice of Nature, now adored,
  Speaks out upon your side.

Tho wepons which your hands hav found,
  Ar those the brain hath wrought—
Light, truth and love ; your battle ground
  The free, broad field of thought.

O may no selfish purpose break
  The beauty of your plan ;
Nor lie, from throne or altar, shake
  Your stedy faith in man.

102. THE MEN WHO WORK.

Tune—Life on the Ocean Wave.

Hurrah for the men who work,
   Whatever their trade may be ;
Hurrah for the men who wield the pen,
   For those who plow the sea ;
And for those who earn their bred
   By th' swet of an honest brow,
Hurrah for the men who dig and delve,
   And they who reap and sow !

Hurrah for the sturdy arm,
   Hurrah for the stedy wil,
Hurrah for the worker's helth and strength,
   Hurrah for the worker's skil,
Hurrah for the open heart,
   Hurrah for the noble aim,
Hurrah for loving quiet home,
   Hurrah for an honest name !

Hurrah for the men who strive,
   Hurrah for the men who save,
Who sit not down, and drink til they drown
   But struggle and brest the wave.
Hurrah for the men on land,
   And they who'r on the sea;
Hurrah for the men who'r bold and brave,
   The good, the true, and the free !

              J. Richardson.

103. OUR FORE-MOTHERS. 8, 7.

Down the vista of the century,
  Through its dim and shadowy years,
Teeming with their toils and struggles,
  Joys and sorrows, hopes and fears,
Comes the voice of noble women,
  Who, with sons and brothers, long
Fought for truth and right the battle—
  Our fore-mothers, brave and strong.

Women who, when freedom, fettered,
  Shook its chains, defiance hurled;
'Twas their hand that lit the beacon,
  Theirs the flag of truth unfurled;
Theirs, the fingers, swift and skilful,
  Spun the flax as white as snow;
Wove the cloth that clothed the armies
  Which for freedom struck the blow.

When the clouds of warfare darkend,
  And the country's woe seemd near,
Their's, the brave hearts, full of curage,
  That the douting helpt to cheer.
Theirs, the hearts that, true and tender,
  Knew no faltering or distrust;
Cheerd the hopeles, soothd the weary,
  With their words of faith and trust.

Women of the nineteenth century,
  With your wond'rus gifts so rare;
Freedom, from all old-time thraldom!
  Freedom now, to do or dare.

Look not on the the great world's conflicts,
  Through your curtain's flimsy lace;
But with heart and hand be doing
  Something to advance the race.

                    Dora Darmore.

---

104. AN EARNEST WIL. C. M.

There's nothing like an earnest wil,
  To struggle through the world,
And to repel the arrows stil,
  By fate against us hurled.

The bourne may be a distant one
  Which we may wish to gain;
Our path may be a weary one
  'Mid sorrow, want, and pain.

But if resolve be stedfast stil,
  'Twil be our guiding ray;
For where there is an earnest wil
  We're sure to find a way.

                    Scott.

---

105.   LIV AND LABOR. 8, 7.

Labor fearles, labor faithful,
  Labor while the day shal last;
For the shadows of the evening
  Soon the sky wil overcast;
Ere shal end thy day of labor,
  Ere shal rest thy manhood's sun,
Strive with every power within thee,
  That th' appointed task be done,

Life is not the traceles shadow,
　Nor the wave upon the beach;
Though our days ar brief, yet lasting
　Is the stamp we giv to each.
Life is real, life is earnest,
　Full of labor, full of thought;
Every hour and every moment
　Is with living vigor fraught.

106,　　LIV TO DO GOOD.　8, 8, 6.

Tune—Ariel.

Liv to do good—this world should be
But one united family,
　One holy brotherhood;
Where each should for his neighbor feel,
Helping along the general weal,
　The universal good.

Liv to do good—an idle wail
Is useles—action must prevail;
　A living pattern teach;
Invoke example's potent aid,
And that to which you would persuade,
　Practice as wel as preach.

Liv to do good—if festering sores
Humanity with tears deplores,
　Strive all you can to heal;
Direct the young, and comfort age,
Boldly for right and truth engage,
　And for the suffering feel.

107. LIV FOR SOMETHING.

8, 7.   *Tune—Nettleton.*

Liv for something, be not idle,
  Look about thee for employ,
Sit not down in useles dreaming—
  Labor is the sweetest joy.
Folded hands ar ever weary,
  Selfish hearts ar never gay,
Life for thee hath many duties—
  Activ be then while you may.

Scatter blessings in the pathway,
  Gentle words and cheering smiles;
Better they than gold and silver,
  With their strife creating wiles.
As the plesant sunshine falleth
  Ever on the grateful earth,
So let sympathy and kindnes
  Gladden wel the darkend hearth.

Hearts there ar cpprest and weary·
  Drop the tears of sympathy;
Whisper words of hope and comfort,
  Giv, and thy reward shal be
Joy unto thy soul returning,
  From this perfect fountain hed;
Freely as thou freely givest,
  Shal the grateful light be shed.

108.   SONS OF TOIL.

7s.   *Tune—Hendon.*

Sons of toil, and daughters true,
To our ranks we welcome you.
This our motto, this our song,—
Set the right against the wrong!

Ye who toiling bear distres,
Join our ranks, and labor bles;
Wage the battle brave and strong,
Fight for right against the wrong.

Ye who weary walk the earth,
Bent with toil—no songs of mirth,
Join our ranks, a mighty throng,—
Strike for right against the wrong.

In the shambles, bought and sold,
Know ye not the power of gold?
Lest ye feel the driver's thong,
Strike for right against the wrong.

When the conflict draweth nigh,
This shal be our battle cry,—
Fruits of toil to toil belong,
Set the right against the wrong!

                              Horace M. Richards.

109. TRUTH IS DAWNING.

8, 7. *Tune—Wilmot.*

Truth is dawning ! see the morning
  Kindled over sea and land !
And the gilded hils ar warning
  That the day-spring may not stand !

Far adown it flows and widens,
  Souls ar lighted by the blaze,
And the distant mountain summits
  Stand transfigured with its rays.

Listen to the acclamation,
  Borne along from steep to steep ;
Nation calling unto nation
  Like the surges of the deep.

Brothers, onward ! lo, our standard
  Soaring in immortal youth ;
We'r the vanguard of the nations,
  Girded with the might of truth !

———

110. THE BIRTH OF TRUTH.

7s. *Tune—Ives.*

Hark, the plains with music sound,
Joy and harmony abound,
Truth is born, let brothers sing
Praises to the new born king.

Peace is come, good wil appears,
Brothers, wipe away your tears ;

Truth for you is here to-day,
Truth that never can decay.

Noble minds, thro' mental night,
Heard the sound and saw the light;
Now the sweet and dulcet strains
Echo gladnes thro' the plains.

Brothers, hail your glorious king !
Richest tribute cheerful bring;
Praise and love Truth's gracious name,
And its boundles good proclaim.

L. Webster.

---

111. TRUTH SHAL MAKE US FREE.

C. M. *Tune— Coronation.*

Come, sound the praise of Truth's fair
    name,
    Sing loud on shore. and sea ;
Its worth has earned undying fame,
    For Truth makes all men free.

Before its lessons grand and bright,
    Nations shal bend the knee,
And captives spring to meet the light,
    For Truth shal make them free.

Though Slavery's dul and rusted chain,
    May tel its time-old plea,
And bind men's souls for gold and gain,
    Yet Truth shal make them free.

Then sing again the joyful song,
  Loud let our praises be ;
For right at last shal conquer wrong,
  And Truth make all men free.

Susan H. Wixon.

112. STAND FOR THE RIGHT

C. M. Tune—Devizes.

Be firm, be bold, be strong, be true,
  And dare to stand alone ;
Strive for the right whate'er ye do,
  Though helpers there ar none.

Nay, bend not to the swelling surge
  Of public sneer and wrong ;
'Twil lead thee on to ruin's verge,
  With current wild and strong.

Stand for the right, tho' falsehood rail,
  And proud lips calmly sneer ;
A poisond arrow cannot wound
  A conscience pure and clear.

Stand for the right, and with clean hands
  Exalt the truth on high ;
Thou'lt find warm, sympathising hearts
  Among the passers by.

Stand for the. right ! proclaim it loud ;
  Thou'lt find an answering tone
In honest hearts, and thou'lt no more,
  Be doomed to stand alone.

113. FRIENDSHIP, LOVE AND TRUTH.

C. M.   Tune—St. Martins.

Three royal spirits walk the earth,
　Our guides where'er we go,
And where their gentle footsteps lead
　There is no human woe.

They smile upon the cradled child,
　They bles the hearts of youth,
And age is mellowed by the tuch
　Of Friendship, Love and Truth.

This sacred band forever more
　Wil guard our thorny way,
And those who follow where they lead
　Can never go astray;

For God has framed our nature such,
　Our childhood and our youth;
And age is mellowed by the tuch
　Of Friendship, Love, and Truth.

---

114. TIME STRENGTHENS RIGHT.

Tune—Duke Street.

Think think not that martyrs die in vain,
　Think not that truth so soon wil fail,
We only break to form again,
　We only bow before the gale.

There groweth up a mighty wil,
  And time wil only give it force;
It tendeth to an object stil,
  Tho' somewhat swerving in its course,

Tho' vengance were the battle-cry,
  And fel revenge first drew the sword;
We seek a nobler victory,
  More firm · in act, more true in word.

And all the failures in the past,
  But make the future more secure;
The triumfs of our cause, at last,
  All bygone sufferings ensure.

Secure in truth, we wait the day,
  As watchers wait the morning light;
The false alone need dred delay,
  For time wil only strengthen right.
                    Robert Nicoll.

                ————

115.   WHAT IS NOBLE?

    8, 7. *Tune—Rousseaus Dream.*

What is noble? That which places
  Truth in its enfranchised wil;
Leaving steps—like angel traces—
  That mankind may follow stil.

E'en though scorn's malignant glances
  Prove him poorest of his clan,
He's the noble, who advances
  Freedom, and the cause of man!

116.   YOUR RELIGION.

7. 6.   *Tune—Webb.*

Let love be your religion;
    Let justice be your aim;
Let all that's good and noble
    Your strict attention claim;
Do always unto others
    As you'd hav done to you;
Whatever you ar doing,
    Be always good and true.

Let truth be in your speeches,
    And wisdom in each word;
Let all your words be gentle,
    Let nothing else be heard;
Be kind to all around you,
    And to yourself be true;
Then wil the world respect you,
    And honor what you do.

J. A. Lindberg.

---

117.   LOVE FOR ALL.   L. M.

Inspired by love may we abstain
From all that givs our neighbor pain,
And every secret wish suppres
That would abridge his happines.

Stil may we feel ourselves inclined
To be the frends of all mankind;
Soothe every grief, each want supply,
And aid their virtue and their joy.

118. BENEVOLENCE. C. M.

May I posses an honest heart,
  Above all selfish ends;
Humanely warm to all mankind,
  And cordial to my frends.

May modest worth, without a fear,
  Approach my open door ;
And may I never view a tear,
  Regardles, from the poor.

With conscious truth and honor, stil
  My actions may I gulde ;
Nor know a dred, but that of il,
  Nor scorn , but that of pride.

Thus may I act a duteous part
  In Nature's social plan ;
Assured, the first of moral laws
  Is—Man do good for man.

---

119. GENTLE WORDS.

C. M. D. *Tune—Brattle Street.*

The roses in the Summer time
  Ar beautiful to me,
And glorious ar the many stars
  That glimmer on the sea ;
But gentle words, and loving hearts,
  And hands to clasp my own,
Ar better than the fairest flowers,
  Or stars that ever shone.

The sun may warm the gras to life,
  The dew, the drooping flower,
And eyes grow bright and watch the light
  Of Autum's opening hour;
But words that breathe of tendernes,
  And smiles we know ar true,
Ar warmer than the summer time,
  And brighter than the dew.

It is not much the world can giv,
  With all its subtle art,
And gold and gems ar not the things
  To satisfy the heart;
But, oh, if those who cluster round
  The sunny home and hearth,
Hav gentle words and loving smiles,
  How beautiful is earth.

————

120.   SYMPATHY. :

C. M.   Tune—Downs.

Let such as feel oppression's load
  Thy tender pity share,
And let the helples, hopeles poor
  Be thy peculiar care.

Go, bid the hungry orphan be
  With thine abundance blest;
Invite the wand'rer to thy gate,
  And spred the couch of rest.

Let him who pines with piercing cold
  By thee be warmed and clad;
Be thine the blisful task to make
  The downcast mourner glad.

Then, pleasant as the morning light,
  In peace shal pass thy days,
And heart-approving, conscious joy
  Illuminate thy ways.

Morrison.

————

121.   THINK GENTLY.

C. M. D.   *Tune—Varina.*

Think gently of the erring one,
  And let us not forget,
However darkly staind by sin,
  He is our brother yet;
Heir of the same inheritance,
  Child of the self-same God;
He hath but stumbled in the path
  Which we in weaknes trod.

Speak gently to the erring one,
  For is it not enough,
That innocence and peace hav gone,
  Without thy censure rough?
It sure must be a weary lot,
  That sin-crusht heart to bear,
And they who share a happier fate,
  Their chidings wel may spare.

122. NO EFFORT FRUITLES.

C. M.   *Tune—Heber.*

Scorn not the slightest word or deed,
    Nor deem it void of power;
There's fruit in each wind-wafted seed,
    Waiting its natal hour.

A whispered word may tuch the heart,
    And call it back to life;
A look of love bid il depart,
    And stil unholy strife.

No act falls fruitles; none can tel
    How vast its power may be;
Nor what results enfolded dwel
    Within it silently.

Work and despair not; bring thy mite,
    Nor care how small it be;
Peace is with all who serve the right,
    The holy, true, and free.

----

123. HOLD THE LIGHT. 8, 7.

Ho! thou traveler on life's highway,
    Moving carelesly along—
Pausing not to watch the shadows
    Low'ring o'er the mighty throng,
Stand aside and mark how feebly
    Some are struggling in the fight,
Turning on thee wistful glances—
    Begging thee to hold the light.

Look! upon the right a brother
  Wanders blindly from the way;
And upon the left a sister,
  Frail and erring, turns astray;
One kind word perchance may save them,
  Guide their wayward steps aright;
Canst thou, then, withhold thy counsel?
  No; but fly and hold the light!

Hark! a feeble wail of sorrow
  Bursts from the advancing throng,
And a little child is groping
  Through the darknes deep and long.
'Tis a timid orfan, shivering
  'Neath misfortune's withering blight!
Friends, home, love, ar all denied her;
  O, in pity hold the light.

124.   SPEAK GENTLY.

C. M.   *Tune—Henry.*

Speak gently, it is better far
  To rule by love than fear;
Speak gently, let no harsh word **mar**
  The good we may do here.

Speak gently to the young, for they
  Wil have enough to bear;
Pass throug this life as best you may,
  'Tis full of anxious care.

Speak gently to the aged one,
  Grieve not the careworn heart;

The sands of life ar nearly run,
  Let them in peace depart.

Speak gently to the erring ones,
  They must hav toiled in vain;
Perchance unkindnes made them so;
  O, win them back again!

Speak gently,—'tis a little thing,
  Dropt in the heart's deep wel;
The good, the joy that it may bring,
  Eternity shal tel.

————

125.   BE KIND. 8, 7.

Ah! be kind—life hath no secret
  For our happines like this;
Kindly hearts ar seldom sad ones,
  Blesing ever bringeth blis;
Lend a helping hand to others,
  Smile tho' all the world should frown;
Man is man—we all ar brothers,
  Black or white or red or brown.

Man is man through all gradations,
  Little recks it where he stands,—
How divided into nations,
  Scattered over many lands.
Man is man by form and feature,
  Man by vice and virtue too.
Man—in all, one common nature
  Speaks, and binds us brothers, too.

126. THE MORN OF PEACE.

7. 6. *Tune—The Watcher.*

The morn of peace is beaming,
  Its glory wil appear;
Behold its early gleaming,
  The day is drawing near;
The spear shal then be broken,
  And sheathed the glittering sword,
The olive be the token,
  And peace the greeting word.

Yes—yes, the day is breaking!
  Far brighter glows its beam;
The nations round ar waking
  As from a mid-night dream;
They see it radiance sheding,
  Where all was dark as night,
'Tis higher—wider spreding
  A boundles flood of light.
                    Mrs. Colburn.

---

127. A NOBLE DEED,

Tune—Auld Laug Syne.

A noble deed, a noble thought,
  A motiv pure and high,
The throbbing of a great warm heart
  Can never, never die;
It shines through all the passing years,
  It lights their trubled flow,
And flings a ray of happines
  Upon the hils of woe.

128. MIND WHAT YOU SAY. C. M. D.

In speaking of a person's faults
  Pray don't forget your own;
Remember those with homes of glass
  Should seldom throw a stone.
If we hav nothing else to do
  But talk of those who sin,
'Tis better we should look at home,
  And from that point begin.

We hav no right to judge a man
  Until he's fairly tried;
Should we not like his company,
  We know the world is wide.
Some may hav faults—and who hav not?—
  The old as wel as young;
Perhaps we may, for aught we know,
  Hav fifty to their one.

I'l tel you of a better plan,
  And one that works full wel;
I try my own defects to cure
  Ere I of others tel.
And, though I hope sometime to be
  No worse than some I know,
My own short comings bid me let
  The faults of others go.

Then let us all, when we commence
  To slander frend or foe,
Think of the harm one word may do
  To those who little know.
Remember curses sometimes like
  Our chickens "roost at home."
Don't speak of others' faults until
  We hav none of our own.

129. DEDICATION HYMN. C. M.

Let monumental pillars rise,
  In majesty sublime,
Their lofty colums shal decay
  Before the tuch of time.

But mind, enlightend and refined,
  Shal soar beyond the sky,
And hev'nly sciences explore,
  Though time itself should die.

This temple now we dedicate
  To Truth's supreme coutrol—
To virtue and progresive thought—
  The riches of the soul.

---

130. EDUCATION. 8, 7.

O for such an education—
  Knowledge prosp'ring in the land,
As shal make this busy nation
  Great in heart as strong in hand.

Knowledge free and unencumberd,
  Bound by no dogmatic cords,
Quick'ning minds that long hav slumberd
  Dubling life by living words.

Knowledge that shal lift opinion
  High above life's drifting sands;
Thought claims limitles dominion—
  Men hav minds as wel as hands.

Shal we wait and wait forever,
  Stil procrastination rue,
Self exertion trusting never,
  Always dream and never do?

Wait no longer—hope, faith, labor,
  Make man what he ought to be;
Never yet .hath gun or saber
  Conquerd such a victory.

---

131. THE COMMON SCHOOL. 8. 7.

The common school, the common school,
  We sing its praise forever;
O not from its ennobling rule
  Can our affections sever.
How memory hallows every hour
  Along its flow'ry mazes,
And consecrates anew each power
  Of thought, to sing its praises.

The common school, a holy charm
  On all its scenes reposes;
Here wisdom stands with open palm,
  To crown us with her roses.
Here mind is might, nor can you buy
  Diplomas here with dollars;
The marks of true distinction lie
  In being earnest scholars.

The common school, O let its light
  Shine through the country's story;

Here lies her welth, her strength, her
    might,
Here rests her future glory.
The past a living witnes stands,
  On all, this truth impresing,
The common school is to our land
  A source of priceles blesing.

---

132. THE VOICE OF WISDOM.

S. M.   *Tune—Dennis.*

Once in the busy streets
  Did Wisdom cry aloud,
And then she perisht 'mid the scofs
  Of a misguided crowd.

Once in the quiet grove
  Did Wisdom's accents charm,
And then she perisht by the blows
  Of conquest's iron arm.

In Palestine and Greece,
  Thus Wisdom's voice was husht,
Yet echo oft the sound renewd
  Though Wisdom's sons were crusht.

But ever in the skies,
  In earth, and sea, and air,
Does Wisdom teach the human heart,
  And none can crush her there.

Systems and teachers change,
  They flurish and decay,
But ne'er from nature's truth and love
  Shal Wisdom pass away.

133.   PATRIOTIC SONG.

Tune—Star Spangled Banner.

Ye sons of Columbia who bravely hav
    fought
For those rights which unstaind from
    your sires hav descended,
May you long taste the blesings your
    valor has bought,
And your sons reap the soil which
    their fathers defended;
    'Mid the reign of mild peace
    May your nation increase,
With the glory of Rome, and the
    wisdom of Greece;
And ne'er may the sons of Columbia
    be slaves,
While the earth bears a plant or the
    sea rolls its waves.

In a clime whose rich vales feed the
    marts of the world,
Whose shores ar unshaken by Europe's
    commotion,
The trident of commerce should never
    be hurld,
To increase the legitimate power of the
    ocean.
    But should pirates invade,
    Though in thunder arrayed,
Let your cannon declare the free
    charter of trade;
      For ne'er shal the sons, etc.

The fame of our arms, of our laws the
    mild sway,
Had justly ennobled our nation in story,
Til the dark clouds of faction obscured
    our bright day,
And envelopt the sun of American
    glory.
But let traitors be told,
Who their country hav sold,
And bartered their God* for his
    image in gold,
      That ne'er shal the sons, etc.
Thomas Payne.

---

134.   SOCIAL LOVE.

L. M.   *Tune—Bonnie Doon.*

For gold-bright suns in worlds above,
    And blazing gems in worlds below,
Our world has Love and only Love,
    For living warmth and jewel glow.

God's Love is sunlight to the good,
    And Woman's, pure as diamond's sheen,
And Friendship's mystic brotherhood,
    In twilight beauty lies between.
Milnes.

---

* NOTE.—Besides designating the primal. evolving
Force of Nature as suggested on page 9, the word
" God " may be considerd as expressing any man's
highest conception of what is noblest and best in the
universe or in humanity—the totality of all GOOD.

135. O CLING TO THE UNION.

Tune—Portuguese Hymn.

O cling to the Union ! that gallant old bark,
Hath rode out the storm when the tempests were dark ;
Her timbers were fram'd by a patriot band,
Who'v past on before to the shadowy land.

O cling to the Union ! for brothers we ar,
We can spare from our flag not a stripe or a star ;
Together united our race let us run,
For our hopes and our aims and our glory ar one.

O cling to the Union ! 'twas purchased with blood,
'Twas wet the tears of the brave and the good ;
The spirits that framed it hav gone to their rest,
And the turf lieth green on each patriot's brest.

O cling to the Union ! the hope of the world ;
Let the flag of the free, on the breeze be unfurld,
Til Liberty's song shal triumfantly roll,
From ocean to ocean, from tropic to pole.

Theodore Wood.

136. FARMER'S SONG. 8. 7.

Earth, of man the bounteous mother,
  Feeds him stil with corn and wine;
He who best would aid his brother,
  Shares with him these gifts divine.

Many a power within her bosom
  Noisles, hidden, works beneath:
Hence ar seed, and eaf and blossom,
  Golden ear and clustered wreath.

These to swel with strength and beauty,
  Is the royal task of man;
Man's a king, his throne is Duty,
  Since his work on earth began.

Bud and harvest, bloom and vintage,
  These like men, ar fruits of earth;
Stampt in clay, a hev'nly mintage,
  All from dust receive their birth.

Barn and mil and wine-vat's tresures.
  Earthly goods for earthly lives,
These ar Nature's ancient plesures,
  These her child from her derives.

Wind and frost, and hour and season,
  Land and water, sun and shade—
Work with these, as bids thy reason,
  For they work thy toil to aid.

Sow thy seed and reap in gladnes!
  Man himself is all a seed;
Hope and hardship, joy and sadnes,
  Slow the plant to ripenes lead.—*Sterling.*

137.   FAITH AND HOPE.

8s.   *Tune—De Fleury.*

O sweet is the season of rest,
  When life's weary journey is done;
The beam that spreds over its west,
  The last lingering ray of its sun.
Tho' dreary the empire of night,
  I soon shal emerge from its gloom,
And see immortality's light,
  Arise on the shades of the tomb.

Then welcome the last hevy sigh,
  When these aching heart-strings shal
    break,
When deth shal extinguish this eye,
  And moisten with dew the pale cheek.
No terror the prospect begets,
  I am not mortality's slave;
The sunbeam of life as it sets,
  Sheds a halo of peace on the grave.

————

138.   MARRIAGE.

Tune—Portuguese Hymn.

When virtue and beauty
  Ar wedded in one,
And strength and true manhood,
  Ar blended with fun;
United together,
  With rapture and song,
The lives will be happy,
  And helthy and long;

With joys of the home,
  A great blesing attends;
It sums up the whole in
  Wife, children, and frends.
Now my benediction
  Unto you is given;
May life here be long,
  And your earth be a heven.

---

139. GATHER YOUR ROSES.

8, 7. *Tune—Shining Shore.*

Gather your roses while you may,
  Old time is ever flying;
And that same flower which blooms to-day
  To-morrow may be dying.

Wisely improve the present hour,
  Be innocently merry,
Slight not the plesures in your power,
  Which wil not, cannot tarry.

Let virtue ever be your guide
  While merged in fleeting plesure;
All other objects else beside,
  Can prove no lasting tresure.

Tho' time must fly, the leaves may fade,
  And all things prove uncertain,
In friendship's path we'l ever tred,
  Till deth shal drop the curtain.

Abner Kneeland.

140.   HARVESTED.

L. M. *Tune—Malvern.*

So ripe and full, the gathered sheaf,
Why should the harvest bring us grief?
Hevy and bent by weight of grain,
Garnered—a life not lived in vain.

Simple his life, to others given,
In duty done, he found his heven—
The burden raised, the dried up tears,
His glorious crown through endles years.

Knowing no color, race, or creed—
His life one prayer of loving deed—
He too, at last, unfettered, free,
Earth's bondage leaves for liberty.

---

141.   WHAT ART THOU DETH?

C. M. *Tune—Arlington.*

What art thou deth, that I should fear
    The shadow of a shade?
What's in the name, that meets the ear,
    Of which to be afraid?

Thou art not care, thou art not pain,
    But thou art rest and peace;
'Tis thou canst make our terrors vain,
    And bid our torments cease.

Thy hand can draw the rankling thorn
  From out the wounded brest;
Thy curtain screens the wretch forlorn,
  Thy pallet brings him rest.

Misfortune's stings, affection's throes,
  Destruction's pois'nous breth—
The world itself, and all its woes,
  Ar swallowed up in deth.

Then let us pass our lives in peace,
  The little time we stay;
Nor let our acts of frendship cease
  Til life shal fade away.

----

142. THEY CANNOT DIE.

L. M. *Tune—Hamburg.*

Say not they die, those martyr souls
  Whose life is wingd with purpose fine;
Who leave us, pointing to the goals;
  Who learn to conquer and resign.

Such cannot die, they vanquish time,
  And fil the world with growing light,
Making the human life sublime
  With memories of their sacred might.

They cannot die whose lives ar part
  Of that great life which is to be;
Whose hearts beat with the world's great
      heart,
  And throb with its high destiny.

LONG METER.

Let all with grateful hearts adore
The great. unknown, eternal Power,
Whose certain laws we seek to know
And then a glad obedience show.

———

To Nature's God let praises flow;
He dwels with men on earth below;
His reign is love—no monarch's throne-
His life in earth and heven ar one.

COMMON METER.

To Science, Truth and Reason, all
    Our heartfelt praise is given;
For they wil bring the reign of **Love**
    And make of earth a heven.

———

To Wisdom, Mercy, Truth and **Love**
    We pay the homage due;
May all the virtues more abound,
    And these our hearts renew.

SHORT METER.

To Wisdom, Power, and Love,
    The God which all adore,
Be glory as it was, is now,
    And shal be evermore!

8, 7.

May the grace of mother Nature,
    And the light of Reason's ray,
With our honest, firm endeavor,
    Guide our feet in Wisdom's way,
        ‖: From it, never :‖
May we heedles turn away.

INDEX OF TUNES.

A large majority of the tunes whose names ar given in connection with the songs of this book, may be found in the ordinary Tune books used in congregational singing.

LONG METER.

PECULIAR METER.

SPECIAL TUNES.

www.ingramcontent.com/pod-product-compliance
Lightning Source LLC
Chambersburg PA
CBHW030620270326
41927CB00007B/1260